CRIMES &
PUNISHMENT
LIFE AS A
CFL OFFICIAL

CRIMES&PUNISHMENT
LIFE AS A CFL OFFICIAL

NEIL PAYNE

Cover design by Doowah Design Inc.
Cover photo by Brian Sytnyk/Vis-U-Tel
Printed and bound in Canada

We acknowledge the financial assistance of the Manitoba Arts Council and The Canada Council for the Arts for our publishing program.

Canadian Cataloguing in Publication Data

Payne, Neil
    Crimes & punishment

Includes index.
ISBN 1-896239-69-2

    1. Payne, Neil 2. Football referees—Canada—Biography.
I. Title. II. Title: Crimes & punishment.

GV939.P386A3 2000   796.335'092   C00-901157-9

Table of Contents

Preface

Reluctantly, I finally realize that this work was inevitable, and a cathartic necessity to rid myself of the cumulative effects of 40 years of scars, and at times self doubts, inflicted by coaches, media, and fans who unfortunately on the odd occasion may have even been right when they questioned the adequacy of my eyesight.

But what a perfect way to end a career, where working in silence was not a choice, but a requirement. The 1999 season was to be my last, but when Ross Perrier, the director of officiating, passed away in October, things changed very quickly.

After the season it wasn't long before Ed Chalupka, vice-president of operations for the league, offered me the director of officiating position. My threat that I wouldn't move to Toronto to do the job didn't have the desired effect as Ed suggested I could do the job out of Winnipeg.

The challenges are immense. Looking for young men in Canada who are capable officiating football at the pro level is like looking for the Holy Grail. Hell, there are more hockey officials in Regina than there are football officials in all of Canada, including Labrador.

Everyone loves a challenge and no professional sports league faces more challenges than the Canadian Football League, particularly if it is to survive over the long term.

My first official duty as director of officiating was to attend the annual Rules Committee in Edmonton, where major changes during the past 20 years were few and far between. Numerous attempts to change any facet of the game, including the elimination of a single point on missed field goals, were quickly punted, usually with little or no discussion, and the mood appeared no different for the first gathering of the millennium.

However after some initial discussion and heated debate, there was a mumbled agreement that perhaps everything was not right with the game, as evidenced by all the empty seats.

The CFL has maintained a death grip on its present format of overtime requiring two additional halves to determine a winner, which in most cases has long been decided before the final whistle, while every other professional league, where possible, has adopted some form of sudden death overtime to provide increased fan excitement and use as a marketing tool.

It was time for a change, but all previous attempts had brought the same inevitable result—nothing. The mood appeared no different as I proposed a format that would distinctly change our format to sudden death, but there was a difference; finally a recognition that changes were required, and after considerable discussion the proposal was passed.

It was the first time in 20 years that the consideration of the fans and the need for marketing and not the needs of the individual teams, were at the top of the list. While the committee recognized that probably further tuning of the overtime rules might be required it was time to take the first step to bring the game into the new century. The new overtime rules better work or I'll have the shortest tenure of any director of officiating on record.

During my real life outside of football I have been successful in avoiding all modern technology, but now I have it all: high-speed modems, computers, e-mail, fax machines, and cell phones all generously supplied by the league and its general managers.

It didn't take along before I realized it was a great conspiracy designed to give coaches and general managers more complete and direct access to complain about all the imaginary missed calls. Now when I decide not to answer the phone because the shrill ring tells me it's Coach Mohns, he simply sends me a fax. When I decide it's time to play solitaire on the computer there is still no escape, as the e-mail sign beats fiercely at the bottom of the screen.

Even a ride in the country is punctuated by the incessant ring of the cell phone, and the coach complaining about Jake Ireland and his crew.

"Coach, Ireland's crew didn't work your last game," I knowingly responded.

I know, but he's working our next game," he complained.

"Shit, now they're complaining about the officials even before the game." I feel like calling the *Guinness Book of Records* because I'm convinced I'm in charge of the largest complaint department of the world.

But all this technology is not without its advantages. My typing skills are less than nil and I have been forced to don a microphone and headset to speak to the computer and even though it frequently rejects my somewhat less than perfect use of the English language, I know if the director of officiating thing doesn't work out I'll be able to use my newfound skills dispensing orders at McDonald's.

The other major reason to complete my story was to thank my wife Gloria and the wives of every husband who ever wore a striped referee's football jersey, and as usual, she is left to the last.

These women are the only people in the world, including the commercial cleaners who call incessantly looking for something to clean, who can get green grass stains out of white pants after we have been knocked to the ground by some overgrown lineman.

Even when we aren't doing a game we are somewhere between Mars and Earth, either thinking about the last game where we should have been better, or getting ready for the next one, leaving them virtual widows with a live-in guest. Well, after 40 years, I'm ready to return and hopefully I'll be able to fit into the real world.

Also an additional special thanks to Gloria, who I dragged into the technology so she could transfer my words onto the computer because no one else could read my writing, including myself. Remarkably, but not surprisingly, she maintained the dignity and composure that she possessed during our 40 years together, never once questioning the material, beyond rolling her eyes, and questioning whether it was suitable for the grandchildren once they turned 18.

1

Why?

Why do it? That's a question put to all officials, whether you are a father umpiring a Little League game and listening to the sharp barbs of the parents who you thought were your friends, or a professional official whose work is constantly being criticized by commentators who have the benefit watching slow motion replays from five different angles of a split second judgment you made looking through someone's legs.

But it could be worse. You could be a South American soccer referee, who after every game is chased by an angry mob of fans to the trap door at the end of the field. He doesn't always make it, and the results can be a severe beating by the fans of the losing team.

In the last 30 years I asked myself "Why?" many times. Usually it was before a game on a holiday long weekend in Regina or Calgary, when I was looking out a hotel room window at either a back alley wall covered with the "F" word; or a sundrenched empty street, with only the occasional piece of newspaper making its way down the sidewalk like a prairie tumbleweed. At that moment, it seemed everyone else was either at the lake with their family or out celebrating Canada Day. What made it worse was that you just left your wife and kids back home having a great time in the pool, or the kids getting ready for an important baseball tournament you wouldn't see.

While being away from your family was an accepted way of life for a Canadian Football League official, public criticism at times could be difficult. If you wanted people to like you, it didn't take long to realize that you were in the wrong business. Most officials accept criticism as part of the game, but reading about it in the paper can take a strip out of even the most grizzled veteran.

In the CFL, an official's only defense to criticism, whether accurate or not, is silence, which makes it doubly difficult to read in the paper about your incompetent officiating when you know you made the right call, or worse, you weren't even involved in the play.

In a game between Winnipeg and Edmonton in 1969, Syd Beckov, a veteran CFL official, was vilified by a radio announcer for a poor call. The announcer questioned everything but Syd's ancestry. As it turned out, not only did Syd not make the call, he wasn't even in the game. Syd also happened to be a lawyer, so for once an official had the last word. After considerable pressure, the radio station publicly admitted its mistake.

Criticism is the one constant that officials must live with, game in and game out. When you are doing a good job, it can easily be ignored, and even be a positive force. In a game in Winnipeg (nothing like causing trouble in your own hometown), our crew was doing a great job when I made a call against the Bombers that was not only right but necessary. The deafening chorus of "Bullshit…bullshit…" by 25 thousand fans sounded like a symphony, because I knew I was right.

Officials are usually their own worst critics and know when they aren't performing; public and media criticism usually only confirms what they already know. At this point self-doubt, fear, and denial take over and "Why am I doing this?" becomes a serious question.

The old adage, you are only as good as your last call, is particularly true after a bad call, when you have to deal with the reality of your own errors, some of which will never be forgotten either by yourself or by those who follow the game. The consequences of a poor call, or even questionable judgments in a tight game, can be devastating for everyone involved, particularly the officials.

In 1984, at an officials' Grey Cup reunion in Edmonton, Pep Moon, a retired old-timer from the Edmonton officials' association, recalled, as if it were yesterday, the 1937 Grey Cup in which Toronto defeated Winnipeg 4–3 on a controversial no yards call late in the game. The call was made by Eddie Grant, a Winnipeg insurance broker. According to Pep, by the time Eddie returned to Winnipeg most of his clients had canceled their insurance policies. Not only did he never officiate again, he was forced to look for work in another province.

I questioned how Pep could accurately remember the details of something that happened almost 60 years ago, when it appeared he might have trouble remembering last week's score. I should have never doubted Pep's account because when Bill Harcourt, a current CFL official, found a copy of a 1963 article by Jim Hunt that included an account of the 1937 Cup incident, it was as if Pep had written the story. The only thing Pep didn't mention was that Bill Ceretti, who scored what would have been the winning touchdown for Winnipeg, went on to become a CFL official, undoubtedly taking up Eddie's vacated seat at the Winnipeg meetings.

When Eddie returned to Winnipeg after the game, he obtained a copy of the game film, which showed his no yards call to be absolutely correct, but no one was even interested in looking at it. The film proved he was right, but in the mind of the Winnipeg fans, Eddie Grant had cost them the Grey Cup and forgiveness was out of the question. No one would talk to him, not even his life-long friends.

Eddie Grant paid the ultimate price for being an honest hometown official at the Grey Cup. It cost him his officiating career, his job, his reputation, and forced him to relocate, all for a $25 game fee. It is a story made more tragic by the fact Eddie was right, which in the end is the only real meaningful measure of an official.

Eddie's misfortunes should have brought an abrupt end to hometown officials working play off and Grey Cup games but it didn't, and those who followed would pay a similar price until the practice was finally discontinued in 1983.

Every official who has ever blown a whistle is forced to deal with his mistakes from time to time, and thankfully most are able to take a deep breath and climb back up the pole. But unfortunately, officials also make mistakes that impact the outcome of a game. In pro sport these mistakes become magnified when they decide a championship or a team's playoff chances. The inevitable pressures and criticism from the media, the teams, the director of officiating, and probably the toughest of all, yourself, can be overwhelming.

Usually, only the best officials are able to manage this type of adversity and return to their former level of officiating, although with a few more emotional scars.

Little did Alan McColman, a six-year CFL official from Hamilton, know of the problems and challenges he would face when he accepted an assignment to officiate the Toronto-Hamilton Eastern final in 1983.

In that game, everything was on the line between two outstanding teams, which had one of the great rivalries in Canadian sport. The feeling was so intense, Hamilton fans would rather give up their Canadian citizenship than consider moving to Toronto. To add to the pressure, Al had the additional burden of working the game with his hometown team.

Everything had gone well for Al until late in the fourth quarter when he made a controversial pass interference call against Hamilton. Not only did the Hamilton fans agree that it was the wrong call, but it cost them the most important game of the year.

Seventeen years later, I contacted Al and apologetically asked if he were prepared to talk about the call. He remembered the play as if it happened yesterday, and the scars that it had left still seemed fresh. Getting directly to the point I asked, "Was it a bad call?"

Without any hesitation he responded, "Probably not, but it was a marginal call that shouldn't have been made."

From the time we start officiating, we are constantly reminded by psychologists, officiating handbooks, supervisors and all of the experts, that if you make a bad call, just forget about it. The question is how? Like Al, I had run into a similar problem and wanted to know how he felt after the call. "I felt totally helpless knowing that I could not change what had happened in that split second," he said. "Even today, it never completely leaves my mind."

I realized that we were sharing feelings that we hadn't even shared with our own wives, let alone with other officials. After I hung up, it occurred to me that perhaps officials were human after all.

When Al returned to Hamilton the problems for his family were just beginning, and even today there are constant reminders. It started with a media feeding frenzy, questioning his competency and even speculating whether he was on drugs. This was followed by an unrelenting barrage of anonymous phone calls threatening his life and warning him, "We know where your kids go to school."

Even today, 17 years later, old wounds are reopened by either a sportscaster or some fan trying to be humorous. I asked Al whether the incident had changed him in any significant way. "After that game," he said, "I was no longer a light-hearted guy. Even today I'm withdrawn with people who I don't know, because inevitably the issue will come up."

But every tragedy has its own humour. The night before I talked to Al, he attended a social function in Hamilton and was quickly cornered by a young couple, who, obvious fans of the CFL, noticed Al's CFL pin.

It didn't take long before they started to tell Al how Hamilton was screwed in the 1983 final by a call made by Jake Ireland. We both laughed. Jake could handle it.

Had you ever considered quitting, I asked?

"No," he said, "it was at the end of the season, and I was young enough to bounce back and show people what I was really all about." But the next year at the officials' clinic, Al appeared sullen and withdrawn. If you had taken a poll, you would have been lucky to find a handful of officials who thought he could make it back. There was no, "Come on Al, you can do it." Or slaps on the back. Everyone knew if he was going to make it, he'd have to do it on his own. It wasn't easy, but after a few stumbles, years of perseverance and a stubborn belief in his own abilities allowed him to shake off his demons.

The CFL record books will tell you Alan McColman is now a 20-year veteran who has worked in eight Grey Cups. What it doesn't say is that he is one of the league's best downfield officials, and from the press box he looks a lot taller than five feet eight inches. As Alan and I laughed about Jake being blamed for Al's questionable call, little did we know that Jake was about to become involved in one of the CFL's biggest controversies, in the most important game of the year, the 1996 Grey Cup.

The league had reached the low point in its history with its financial problems dominating the sports pages and its survival looked questionable. An exciting and controversy-free Grey Cup seemed essential if the game was to have any chance of replacing the league's problems on the sports pages.

Unfortunately, our officiating performances in the several previous Grey Cups were less than adequate. Ross Perrier became director of officiating in 1995, and Don Barker, who he replaced, and myself, both now league supervisors, discussed the problem at the end of the 1995 season. Why weren't we getting the job done in recent Cups? Was it the pressure of the game, or the excitement and hype of the week that was distracting the officials? We didn't know, but decided to bring the officials in later in the week in the hope of repeating their preparation for the playoffs, where we had been so successful.

There was one single message Ross preached in our pre-game preparation. Make sure the play is over before you blow your whistle, then put the ball down and get out of the players' way, and make sure if you make a call that it's a good one.

Weather, which always seems to be a factor at outdoor Grey Cups, reared its head. A few hours before the game it started to snow extremely large wet flakes, which soon covered the field. I knew it was the Grey Cup because even though Hamilton had two snow sweepers it wasn't long before we found one had hydraulic problems and was virtually useless. But we had hoardes of Hamilton workers equipped with corn brooms. I was in charge at field level and keeping the sidelines and numbers clear, as well as the major lines, was not a problem, but I still wonder if the cash-strapped league ever collected from its sponsors, whose logos at centre field remained covered during the game.

It was a Grey Cup Classic, which is a lofty statement considering the history of outstanding games that had come before. The underdog Eskimos matched the Flutie-led Argos stride for stride. Flutie had to be at his best, and he was, as Edmonton scratched and clawed with shoe-top catches and the Gizmo's incredible kick returns on the snow-covered the field.

We were playing the Canadian final in a winter setting in an outdoor stadium, with the game still in doubt late in the fourth quarter, and with fans from all across the country having a great time. It was a day you knew what it meant to be a Canadian. It couldn't get any better. Even the officials were doing a great job.

With less than five minutes to go, the game was still in doubt. Toronto was leading 33-30 and driving toward the Edmonton goal line. The snow was still falling, large flakes floating onto the field. The scene and the mood of the crowd made it seem more like Christmas than a Grey Cup.

Suddenly Toronto had a decision to make. It was third and one. Should they gamble and put the game out of reach, or try a field goal? In Canadian football there is no choice. You gamble. I moved along the sideline near the first down marker to get a better look. Flutie tried to hand off to Robert Drummond, and almost immediately the ball was at referee Jake Ireland's feet in the offensive back field. Then a whistle killed the play. I thought, Jake, how could you blow your whistle when the ball was on the ground? To make matters worse, Edmonton recovered the ball. But we still had a chance. Toronto hadn't made it back to the line of scrimmage and was short of a first down. Edmonton would still get the ball.

But in officiating, when things go wrong, they really go wrong. Ross Saunders, the umpire, marked the forward progress beyond the line of scrimmage. A measurement was required, and sure enough, Toronto had a first down by inches. They moved in to score and take control of the game.

I had made my share of mistakes as an official, but I never felt sicker than when I heard that whistle. How could Jake have blown it? Ron Lancaster, the Edmonton head coach, perplexed and totally frustrated, was jumping up and down at the Edmonton bench. I couldn't blame him. After the game, I had to skirt by Coach Lancaster and a gaggle of media who had gathered to hear him crucify the officials.

During the year I had had weekly contact with coach Lancaster, who was one of the few coaches who took the time to critique the officials who worked his games, even though he claimed nothing ever changed: they were always lousy.

I shuddered to think of what he was going to say, all of which was justified, and might just put one of the final nails in the CFL coffin. Instead, Coach Lancaster took the high road and gave full credit to Argos for their win, claiming that even if Edmonton had got the ball, Toronto still would have found a way to win. Instead of burying the league and officials who were already down in the mud, he diffused the controversy with his comments. Despite his deep personal disappointment, and he is one of the most competitive men I have ever met, he raised himself and the league to a higher level.

Why? Ron Lancaster was American-born, but he had spent 20 years in the CFL as a player, colour commentator, and coach, investing his life and his family's future in the Canadian game. In spite of his own anguish, there was no way he would damage the league and the game he loved. It may well have been his finest hour.

In silence, Ross, Don, and I returned to the hotel for a post-game wind up with the officials, which was usually a happy affair, celebrating the year's successes. The mood at the hotel, even with the consumption of Mr. Labatt's products, was like a wake at the death of a close friend.

Maybe we would at least find out why Jake blew the call. The looks on the faces of the officials told us it wasn't Jake who blew the whistle, but rather Ross, who mistakenly thought Drummond had the ball.

To make matters worse, a rookie in the CFL office, who obviously knew nothing about mixing officials and players, had booked the Eskimos and the officials in the Royal Connaught Hotel. Several hours after the game a group of Edmonton players confronted the officials on the hotel elevator in what could have been an ugly situation. Thankfully, after a short but very tense face-to-face meeting, the obviously agitated players got off the elevator with only looks that could kill. Perhaps the Edmonton players really were an extension of their head coach.

The next morning I was eye-to-eye with Coach Lancaster in the hotel lobby. I wanted to apologize for what happened, but it wasn't the time. We exchanged a strained greeting as we quickly passed each other.

Several months later, I finally found the right moment to apologize for what happened. It was during the coach of the year dinner in Edmonton. Even in private Coach Lancaster's attitude hadn't changed. "You have to live with the fact that both players and officials make mistakes," he said, still with no outward bitterness. However, three months later I received his first report for the 1997 season and his criticism of officials hadn't changed. His comments seemed more vociferous than ever, and they were sometimes even accurate.

After the Grey Cup, Jake was faced what many officials before him had known, as well as those who would follow: national criticism for a call he didn't make, followed by his forced silence in accordance with league policy. Even though Coach Lancaster's comments had dulled the criticism, Jake was still identified as the official who blew the early whistle that cost Edmonton any possible chance of winning.

The media pressured Jake, who was sworn to silence by the league, for a statement. He was unable even to say it wasn't he who blew the whistle. Ross Perrier said the league contemplated making a statement clearing Jake of any wrongdoing, but by the end of the week it was old news and the urge passed. With the exception of a small article in an obscure Ontario paper, the world continued to believe Jake screwed Edmonton.

Two years later, Jake was back working the Grey Cup in Winnipeg. At half time I wandered into the officials' dressing room to see if the crew needed anything.

"How's it going," I asked.

"I had a hell of a time getting started," he said.

I thought nothing more of Jake's comments knowing that all officials experience the same problem from time to time, even veterans. A month later I called Jake to talk about the Grey Cup whistle in Hamilton, now that it was a thing of the past. The conversation wasn't much different than the one I had with Al McColman only weeks earlier.

"Did you ever think of quitting because the league didn't come forward and say you hadn't blown the whistle?" I asked.

"I thought about it," he said, "but not seriously. I was only concerned whether I had lost my credibility with the players and teams." It was the answer I had expected from a guy who was probably the league's best referee.

I realized Jake's problems getting started in the Winnipeg Grey Cup were a hangover from the Hamilton game two years earlier. This was a man who refereed more games in the modern history of the Cup than any other official, and who was as mentally tough as any official I had ever met, still living with a mistake he didn't make.

Suddenly the scars and my own demons that I acquired in my 20 years in the league didn't seem so unusual, and I no longer worried that they were the product of some imagined character flaw.

Like Jake and Al, I had the opportunity to live through the experience of the media wringer more than once, the most memorable occurring in a game I refereed in Calgary on a sunny September afternoon in 1979. The visiting Bombers were at the bottom of the league, but were clearly out-playing the less-than-prepared Stampeders. Still, late in the game the Stamps were leading 28-23. With two minutes remaining, Calgary was forced to kick from their 35. Leo Ezerins, a gigantic Winnipeg linebacker, came through unblocked. When he jumped into the air to block the punt, he virtually blocked out the sun and completely covered Mike McTague, the Calgary kicker. There was no way the kick wasn't going to be blocked, but miraculously the Calgary kicker kicked the ball underneath Ezerins, shanking it off to the side across the line of scrimmage. My flag was out in the split second for contacting the kicker, and gone was any chance for a Winnipeg victory.

It would have been easier not to throw the flag because it was impossible to believe that McTague had kicked the ball without it being touched, but I was in a perfect position to see what happened.

After the crew showered, Don King, the league supervisor of officials, returned from the press box to discuss the game with the crew. I could tell by the look on his face that there was a problem. "Neil, what did you see on the last punt?" he asked.

I told Don that somehow the Calgary kicker got the ball away without it being touched.

Don persisted. "I just talked to Don Wittman of the Canadian Broadcasting Corporation who replayed the play several times and he said the film clearly shows that the ball was touched, and the referee blew the call."

Already exhausted from the game, I felt the remaining life drain from my body. How could I have blown the call? I was in a perfect position to see the play.

I was scheduled to fly home with the Bombers, which would have been like waving a red flag in front of a bull, so I called my wife Gloria to tell her I would be taking a later flight.

It was one of the few times she had watched a game and tried to tell me that Wittman was wrong. I knew she knew very little about contacting the kicker rules, and I suspected she was trying to soothe my wounded feelings, so I quickly cut her off.

The crew headed for Chinese food, a rewarding and necessary experience because I was always too nervous to eat before the game. As we waited to order, my thoughts were preoccupied with the blown call. Soon the smell of the Chinese food, usually a welcome aroma, was beginning to make my stomach turn. I needed some fresh air and I needed to be alone.

I sat on the bench outside the restaurant replaying the play over and over again. If I hadn't been in a perfect position to see it, then missing the call may have been understandable. But I saw the whole thing. If you can't get it right when you're looking directly at it, maybe it was time to retire. The fresh air didn't seem to be helping. No wonder, I was oblivious to the grease that was covering my body from the restaurant's nearby exhaust fan. It was time to head for the men's room and clean out my body from both ends.

I wouldn't get a chance to see the play until Monday night, but the jury was already in. When I went for coffee the next morning with 200 other civic workers, it was obvious they were all Bomber fans, and had watched Don Wittman and the CBC. There were comments that shouldn't be repeated in mixed company, along with the usual behind the back finger-pointing and sarcastic laughter. Gloria didn't fare much better on her Monday morning trip to Safeway, with her newfound acquaintances happy to point out her husband's shortcomings. It was also the first time our daughter Leslie found out what it really meant to have a father who referees in the CFL.

By Monday evening my best year as a referee in the league had quickly turned into a low point in my life. Then I finally had a chance to see the play on the supper sports news. At first, I was afraid to look. They showed the play several times including in slow motion. Gloria was right. The replay didn't show Ezerins touching the ball. I knew I should have listened to her. But there was little I could do. The CBC had spoken. I would have to suffer in silence, but that was secondary because now I knew I was right and my confidence had been restored.

The next day I picked up the Free Press and couldn't believe the large black headlines "Referee Payne deserves the benefit of the doubt." John Robertson, a colleague of Don Wittman at the CBC and a *Free Press* sports writer had taken Wittman to task over his comments. Robertson asked, "Did referee Neil Payne blow the big call, or did CBC's Don Wittman blow it?"

Robertson came to the same conclusion as I did. You simply couldn't tell, but "Neil Payne had a better view of the play than any of the people who are trying to crucify him today." It was a direct shot at Wittman's analysis of the play. I wanted to phone John and thank him for his support, but again league policy got in the way and I remained silent.

It wasn't long before I ran into Don Wittman. I was sitting at a nearly empty table at a Winnipeg Jets Golf tournament with Louis Mainella, a close friend who is always willing to share his thoughts, when Don asked if he could join us. Louis promptly told him, "There's no room," and Wittman moved on. I was embarrassed. I hope Witt was too, but I know better.

As luck would have it, I soon met John Robertson at a hockey benefit. John, like myself, was a product of Jesuit schooling, which explained his clear and independent thinking. After I introduced myself and thanked him for his column, I fully expected we'd discuss the call, but it didn't happen. Instead, he lamented about the incredible abuse of power by the media who can turn fiction into fact and crucify people without recourse. It was a lesson that every pro official whoever blew a whistle eventually learned.

On that controversial play, the Calgary kicker, Mike McTague, claimed Leo never touched the ball. But only Leo knew for sure. In the off-season after the Hearns-Leonard fight, I bumped into Leo in one of the local watering holes where, after a few drinks, only the truth is spoken. Leo was so big that it was impossible for him to hide and I headed directly towards him. He knew what was coming. "Leo, did you touch that ball?" I demanded.

"I think so," he replied.

"Leo, that's not good enough. Did you touch it or not?" But he couldn't come up with a better answer. Either he touched the ball and didn't want to hurt my feelings, or Mike McTague and I were right. We'll never know, but at least I can go to the grave believing I was right.

So why would anyone want to be an official? In pro sport today the first thing you hear it is, show me the money! Ask an official how much money he makes, and before you finish asking the question, he'll tell you he isn't doing it for the money. What he is really saying in most cases is that I'm too embarrassed to tell you how little I make. Truly, we don't do it for the cash, but not many would take the abuse without it.

How much? When I started in 1960 in minor football our game fees were $3 per game, and on a weekend you could work three games for a grand total of $9, less about $8 for gas. If you washed your own shoe laces instead of buying new ones you didn't go home broke. Hey, no one said we were smart.

In contrast, when I refereed my last game in the CFL in 1995, I made about $500 per game, with the average game fees in the range of $300, which is still pretty nominal since it can take two or three days of an official's time to work the game, when preparation and travelling time are taken into account.

Officials' game fees in the CFL have gotten considerably better in recent years, not because they have received more money, but rather players' salaries have been substantially reduced, and no longer bear any resemblance to the obscene salaries paid athletes in other sports. In reality, the relationship between CFL players and officials' salaries is probably close to where it should be, recognizing officials are never paid enough for the job they are asked to do, although full-time officials in the NBA, NHL and major league baseball have made substantial gains in recent years, but usually not without bitter and difficult negotiations.

A number of people get into officiating because they want to put something back into the game. For me, altruism was at the bottom of the list. I enjoyed playing all sports, but playing football was my passion. Yet I soon realized that I'd make a better official than player. My insignificant and even shorter playing career either consisted of my coming off the field holding my nose, which quite frankly was a large and easy target, or standing on the sideline pleading, "Now coach?"

My one moment of glory was throwing a TD pass in a university game against Medicine Hat. But that was soon erased by a defensive lineman who successfully planted me head first into the ground without digging a hole. After a rather large headache that seemed to last forever, I correctly concluded football was a dumb game.

While a number of amateur players find their way into officiating, few former professionals in the modern era take up the challenge. Among the exceptions are Tommy Ford, Kas Vidruk, John Stroppa, Bill Jones, and Brian Donnelly, all of whom benefited from their "feel" of the professional game.

In 1986, in a continuing effort to improve the level of officiating in the league, Don Barker, the director of officiating, attempted to attract former professional players who he thought might have a chance to succeed at the pro level. The players were a lot smarter than we thought. They all refused. Their responses ranged from "No way," to a mild interest that quickly disappeared when they learned they would have to start over again and pay the price of serving their apprenticeship in amateur football.

The most compelling motivation is contained in a variety of components, which most officials will deny they possess, some of which are necessary if an official is to succeed at the pro level. The most important tool is an ego (not too large), perhaps better defined as an unfailing confidence in your own abilities, as well as the need to be in charge, facing the challenge, game in, game out; and finally, the desire to be in the public spotlight, no matter how misplaced. These factors can be a recipe for success, but in large doses or out of balance they are guarantees for failure.

Paul Dojack, probably the most famous and heckled referee in CFL history (which is an obvious sign of respect), was always clearly in charge, marching up and down the field like the "Little General" barking out instructions while becoming a public figure more recognizable than the players.

Al Dryburgh, who was as good as any referee I ever worked with, knew it. His career spanned the late '60s and through the '70s, and we used to affectionately refer to him as the NBC Peacock of the CFL.

Unfortunately, Al's uncompromising attitude led to a parting of the ways with the league as he attempted to improve the Oliver Twist working conditions of his fellow officials. In the end we were all losers, but who else but a referee would take on the league alone?

The most recognizable of today's officials is Jake Ireland. His combined record for longevity and Cup appearances as a referee already place him among the league's officiating elite over its 90 year history. Jake's success, while partly due to his considerable ability, directly related to his unflinching belief in himself, a trait which separates the very good from the average official, particularly in tight situations. Yet it is often this very strength that also can be an Achilles heel. Perhaps it's his red hair, but it's not unusual to see Jake waving his finger in the nose of a player or coach while giving them a lecture, sometimes creating rather than solving a problem.

For myself, I thought the reasons for being an official were rather simple. Like most men I loved sports, and what better opportunity to remain a perpetual kid than officiate football? But when I looked in the mirror some 30 years later, the why becomes more evident. Besides the obvious love of doing it, the need to be in charge has dogged me all my life. I was that obnoxious kid who used to organize the local baseball team, tell everyone what position to play, set the ground rules and drive everyone crazy, and then grow up and do the same thing to all your buddies on the golf course. What better way to take charge than become an official, better yet a referee. Think about it—absolute power!

In today's world, no one has the final word. You don't like your boss's decision, you can grieve to the union; convicted in court, appeal it to the Supreme Court; don't like the ruling, then change the law. In sports, justice is swift, particularly in football, where the deed is instantly judged, the sentence pronounced, and the penalty applied. The total process takes less than 90 seconds without appeal, or plea bargain, with the exception of the on-again off-again replays in the NFL.

Fortunately, an official's awesome power is balanced by the constant review and evaluation of his work, by the coaches, media, fans, and supervisors. Responsibility in handling absolute authority brings with it its own associated pressures, which many are not able to handle, particularly when decisions have to be made in a split second, many times with less than conclusive evidence.

And yes, I've enjoyed the public spotlight, although probably it should be more accurately described as notoriety. Why I'm not sure, because inevitably it was used to expose my shortcomings. I'm forced to conclude that my Catholic upbringing and time spent with the Jesuits created the need for me to do public penance.

Late in the 1997 season I was making my way up to the press box when I felt a tug at my sleeve. It was Dancing Gabe, the Bombers friendly cheerleader. "Aren't you Neil Payne?" he asked.

Straightening my shoulders I responded, "That's right. How did you know?" I expected instant recognition, instead he said, "Your name's on your bag."

If you were to ask an official and a coach how important an official was to a football game, responses would be light years apart, but in reality, an official is probably twice as important as a coach thinks he is, but only half is important as he thinks he is.

2

Life in the Minors

After the why, the most asked question is how did you get started? Like many Canadians who end up in a job or profession, it was being in the wrong place at the right time. While attending the University of Manitoba, I saw a sign on the bulletin board advertising for football officials for the inter-faculty program, and better yet, you would be paid. Perfect. Like every student I was desperate for cash and thought I could handle the job.

I hustled down to the sports office hoping the line wouldn't be too long, and that I'd get a chance. It was as if they were handing out typhoid shots; only one other student showed. I had all the work I could handle. It didn't take long to realize that I loved officiating, and I was good at it (there goes that damn ego again). However the memories of university and football officiating were soon replaced by the realities of getting established in the real world, and the mating ritual of the North American male.

Several years later, one of my friends, Jake Scheirich, had joined the Manitoba Football Officials' Association, and asked me if I were interested. Interested! I could hardly wait, but there was a problem. It was 1961 and Gloria and I had been married for only two years and we had two kids. We were playing by the Catholic rulebook, so more children seemed inevitable.

We had agreed at my insistence not to buy a car and save every penny we could for a down payment on a house before the ever-increasing cost of milk eliminated any chance of escaping our ever-shrinking apartment.

How could I convince her to buy a car? Perhaps even more difficult to explain was how, after being away all week at work, I'd be away on weekends officiating, and she would be stuck looking after the kids alone.

After considering a number of devious strategies, I chose the straight-ahead approach and put my heart on the table. Her response was almost immediate. "If that's what you really want, do it." Besides being very supportive, she secretly concluded that if I was away for seven days a week, perhaps the Payne production line would slow down. (But it didn't).

Officials' wives are asked to sacrifice much, whether it's attending one of your relative's weddings who she doesn't know alone, or sitting in the backyard on a long weekend while everyone else is gone to the lake or having a barbecue; or wandering through K-mart on a Saturday night because there is nothing better to do.

I sometimes wonder what Gloria's answer would have been had she known what she faced for the next 35 years. Yet I know her answer would have been the same, and that without our families' support there would be no officiating careers, and we'd all be forced to grow up.

I finally bought that car on our very limited finances. What a deal; $50 for a 1950 Austin. No wonder it was such a bargain. It wouldn't go! But thankfully, after $15 for a head gasket, we were on our way. It didn't take long to realize that the brakes were almost gone, which required frequent warnings about oncoming obstacles.

But the car was ideally suited for the purpose, as most amateur football fields were generously surrounded with additional land, which afforded the opportunity to bring the vehicle to smooth albeit time-consuming stop. In addition, its small size was ideally suited for avoiding stones fans may have been tempted to throw in its direction.

Many believe officials belong to a secret society that meets once a month in the basement of the Elk's Building, which is partly true. But we do relocate on a regular basis, I presume to avoid any potential bomb threats. My application to join the Manitoba Football Officials' Association in 1961 required the sponsorship of two officials, followed by the close scrutiny of my background at the first general meeting, where happily I was put on probation. Contrast this with today, where associations are almost forced to kidnap potential officials off the street, because they are unable or unwilling to put in the time and commit-ment required to become an official.

Little did I realize when I attended that first meeting that the room was filled with lawyers, doctors, teachers, meat packing workers and businessmen, who were all also highly dedicated officials. I've never been associated with a group of individuals before or since that showed more passion and dedication for what they were doing, without concern for personal gain. Once you put on the striped jersey and stepped on the field you left your personal credentials behind and were judged by your performance. More often than not, the butcher commanded more respect than the lawyer, which I guess shouldn't come as a surprise.

The pride was clearly evident at the end of the year, when the annual report indicated every officiating appointment had been filled, knowing officials had worked when they were sick or taken time off work or canceled appointments to work in an early high school game or to take an out-of-town game. By today's standards, our early dedication would be considered fanatical. The dress code required that we wear a standard official's shirt and hat and anything we could get underneath, which eliminated any winter wear including gloves, toques, etc., which are now routinely worn by all officials.

I can recall one particularly cold playoff game in Fort Garry, Manitoba, where by the end of the third quarter I could no longer catch the ball because my hands were permanently frozen in an open position. I knew if the ball hit the ends of my fingers they would shatter. I think our Spartan dress code was to show that we truly were a special breed. But to all the players and the fans wrapped up in their parkas it confirmed what they already knew: we were crazy!

For the next several years, my faithful Austin and I were constant companions, traveling from field to field learning my trade. I was in heaven. One of the highlights for amateur officials was to work the Bomber yardsticks. Not only did we have the best seat in the house, but we got paid. In 1962 we were required to wear white starched shirts when we worked on the sticks, which for my first game received far more meticulous attention than the one I was married in. Calgary was in town to play the Bombers and the air at ground level prior to the game was electric. You could feel the adrenaline growing in both the crowd and at the Winnipeg bench as the clock clicked down to kick off.

The energy and emotion generated by the crowd resembled that of the early crusades, and only the total defeat of the visiting enemy was acceptable. The fans were committed to their warriors, body and soul.

This is in contrast to today's sophisticated fans who view football as one of the many available entertainment choices, perhaps explaining to a large extent the declining interest in the CFL.

As I stood wedged between the sideline and the Bombers' bench, tightly hanging onto my yardstick, I was caught up in the incredible excitement. I vowed then that I would someday become a CFL official. It was a commitment I dared not share with any of my fellow officials, because of the justifiable ridicule that would follow. In reality, only 30 citizens in a country of 20 million would get that chance at any one time. The odds weren't great.

My dream was almost short-lived as I watched the opening kick off float end over end to the Calgary goal line. Out of the corner of my eye, I caught Winnipeg No. 32, Henry Janzen, being blocked out of bounds directly at me. I had nowhere to go. Henry crashed into my yardstick, tumbled to the ground, and of course got tangled up in the chains. My heart was pounding. Henry quickly jumped to his feet and tried to run down the sideline, chain in tow. I dutifully followed behind, desperately trying to shake the chain loose from Henry's legs, which thankfully happened just before we reached the other end of the Winnipeg bench. Thank God! But it wasn't over. I could feel something piercing through the back of my skull. I shouldn't have turned around. It was the steely grey-eyed stare of an up close Bud Grant, the Bomber head coach. He didn't say a word. He didn't have to.

Thankfully my presence was required downfield where referee Paul Dojack was frantically waving first down with no sticks in sight. I finally arrived on the scene, only to notice that my yardstick was bent in a perfect right angle. Like coach Grant, Mr. Dojack was not impressed, but after some fancy knee and foot-work, we were back in business.

For the next seven years my efforts were devoted to officiating and getting into the CFL. Working the Bomber sticks I was only three feet from crossing the sideline and fulfilling that dream. But I was convinced it would've been easier scaling the Berlin wall than getting an opportunity to work as a CFL official. There were very few changes to the CFL staff, yet I was convinced as I watched from the sideline year after year that I could do a better job than some of the officials whom I believed were veterans of the world war, and I don't mean the second.

The road would, indeed, be a long one. The many pressures of pro sport: media and league scrutiny, the incredible speed of the game at the pro level, the skill of the players, and the necessity to officiate consistently at a professional level required a long transition. Even after I made it across, it would take a long time before I could say I was comfortable officiating in the CFL. I realized that the officials I had criticized from the safety and comfort of the other side of the white line were every bit as good as those of us who would follow.

My introduction into the CFL coincided with the increased use of films and television exposure, which led to a more sophisticated and complex game, as well as providing tools for improving officiating, specifically game films for evaluation, and complex teamwork by officials to help cover the play. Other than basic positioning, our predecessors possessed few of our sophisticated tools. Their role more closely resembled that of a western sheriff and his deputies who were hired to maintain law and order, where a gun would have been more useful than a rule book.

Annis Stukus, a Hall of Famer, not only coached and played in the CFL but was also chiefly responsible for organizing both the Edmonton Eskimos and the B.C. Lions. One of our country's true sports icons and treasures, he recalls that, "In the good old days, when players had a disagreement the referee would turn his back on the next play and the combatants would hammer the heck out of each other. After the play was over the referee would run by and say 'Okay boys, let's get back to football'," which ended their disagreement. Today similar action would undoubtedly result not only in penalty flags, but continuing close scrutiny by both officials and TV cameras, as well as league fines.

The game was far more brutal than today's sanitized version, which is played on artificial turf. Back then, the officials job often began after the whistle. When a player was tackled, it was the signal for the rest of his teammates to join in and hopefully remove one of the ball carrier's limbs while he was still on the ground.

"Stuke" recalled a game when he was playing with the Argos. "I got tackled in front of the Ottawa bench and the tackler tried to twist my leg off. He forgot I had another leg and I kicked him in the face to remind him that I knew what he was trying to do, which brought the Ottawa players off their bench. Art West, a teammate who was injured, started to beat the Ottawa players with his crutches. We had a donnybrook." A riot squad would have been more appropriate than the three officials who struggled to restore order.

Maintaining law and order was not confined to between the white lines. Most coaches were just as tough as their players and would just as soon meet the referee in the tunnel or alley as yell at him on the field. Thankfully in the so-called modern era in which I worked, abuse by coaches was verbal in nature, although I'm sure my legs saved me from more than one physical confrontation.

Although most coaches are self-taught experts in psychological warfare and verbal abuse of officials, Bud Riley, coach of the Winnipeg Blue Bombers, and Ron Meyer, coach of the short-lived Las Vegas Posse, were in a class by themselves. They brought into question every part of your being, including but not limited to your eyesight, judgment, family heritage, anatomy, integrity, and intestinal fortitude, in vile and descriptive passages previously not heard on this planet. Every year Webster's Dictionary publishes a set of new words. Riley and Meyer could collaborate on a total volume of new words relating to the performance and abilities of officials.

I knew I was blind, because I was reminded of my ailment. But Coach Riley provided the rationale. "Payne, you're blind because you masturbate all the time," an assessment he shared with many other officials.

In the pursuit of our dreams, it's often the journey, no matter how long or difficult, that provides us with the most satisfaction and reward. I worked my butt off for eight long years waiting for a call from the CFL until I began to doubt it would ever come. Everyone has their own story of hardship, whether it's walking to school in your bare feet or throwing away your crutches to become a star when everyone said you would never walk again. I wish I could tell you mine. The problem is I don't have one.

Those eight years as an amateur official were incredible. The learning curve was almost vertical. Football officiating is unique in that professionals and amateurs work together as members of a local association. On a Saturday night I'd watch Al Dryburgh, Kas Vidruk, Abe Kovnats and George Eakin officiate the CFL game on TV, then join them the next day to work a junior game, listening about the calls they made the night before. What an experience.

The competition among rookies was fierce with everyone struggling to be the best, many with the same dream as mine. However the special bond we developed in working as a team to provide the best officiating possible, made all our ambitions seem secondary.

When I finally got into the CFL, I was joined by Gord Johnson, Bud Ulrich, and Ken Lazaruk. We knew we wouldn't have made it without each other's help, as well as the other amateur officials who, hopefully, would also get their chance.

Football, whether as a player or official, can expose and even shape your personality. In my years as an amateur official I learned more about myself than frankly I wanted to know. The sharp corners of my protruding ego were quickly rounded by the men I worked with (well almost), and I soon learned that only total commitment and effort were good enough if you're going to match the dedication of the players and coaches who spent the last ounce of their energy between the white lines in every game.

The game has its own built-in corrective devices, where any snow-balling thoughts of grandeur were quickly punctuated by a blown call, reminding us of our own shortcomings as well as how difficult the job can be.

But hey, how else could you get out at 7 a.m. on a Saturday morning and not get back until early Sunday? A dream weekend started with the bantam game Saturday morning, then frantically racing across town to do a midget game in the afternoon, and finally off to the stadium to work the yardsticks at the Bomber game, the highlight of the day. Usually you arrived home by midnight but I remember one night arriving later, much later. As usual, the local brewery had left their product in the dressing room for the pleasure of the CFL officials after the game, and as usual the stick crew sneakily, if not skillfully, removed its share and stashed it away for a similar purpose.

Officials, whether amateur or professional, are their worst critics, and the stick crew's assessment of the officials' less than stellar performance that night far out lasted the supply of beer. When we finally packed up our gear and left the dressing room we discovered we were locked in.

Stadiums are designed to keep the non-paying customers on the outside. I can also verify that when the gates are locked they are no less effective in keeping people inside. The task of scaling the ten foot fence after a few beers with equipment slung over your shoulder was a daunting one, but no more formidable than trying to convince the men in blue that you were trying to break out and not in.

When I returned home, Gloria was in bed, but as usual not asleep. I weakly asked, "I wonder if..." and before I could finish she sharply retorted, "Yes," and by early next morning my only striped shirt and pants were again cleaned and pressed lying neatly by my bag for Sunday afternoon's game, and the cycle continued for eight glorious years.

In my first year, I worked 45 games, and after deductions for running the association, the annual wind up and equipment, I was left with almost $35 for Christmas presents for the family. I couldn't have been happier. Imagine getting paid for what you love to do.

My first eight years as an amateur official were undoubtedly the most satisfying and rewarding of my career. Unlike the pro game, which by its very nature is a business, amateur football is infested by people who simply love the game, and who do everything to promote it, which in Canada is a difficult task. It wasn't unusual for a coach to thank the officials after the game for doing a good job, or to offer to take care of a player that was giving us a hard time.

Officials were no different and I had lots of help particularly from Al Dryburgh and Abe Kovnats, two CFL officials who were instrumental in my development and in providing me the opportunity to eventually work the CFL, even though they knew it might eventually cost them their jobs.

Some of that help came in surprising ways. I'd been officiating for only three years and luckily had the opportunity to work as a head linesman on a senior league game, which comprised former pros and graduated juniors, which at that time was the best amateur ball in the country. My second assignment, again on the sideline, was at a game in Steinbach, Manitoba, with three CFL officials, Al Dryburgh, Tommy Ford and Kas Vidruk. During the drive to Steinbach there was the usual horsing around, with Tommy Ford entertaining us with his personal experiences, which were far too hilarious and outrageous to be anything but true.

When we arrived at the field, Tommy instructed me to get my stick crew ready and make sure they knew what their duties were. Hell, it was so difficult to get anyone just to hold sticks, I was happy if they could count to three. Just prior to kick-off, we gathered around in a circle at centre field for our final pep talk before running to our positions. Only this time it was different. Tommy grabbed me by the arms, and Kas slipped the referee's red armband up and over my elbow, looked me in the eye and said, "Payne, you're in charge." With that they all turned and ran to their positions and waited for the opening kickoff. They had thrown down the gauntlet. You think you're good? Let's find out.

I looked over to the sideline where I should have been standing for the opening kickoff, only to find Tommy standing there with my stick crew grinning from ear-to-ear. The adrenaline produced was directly proportional to what you'd expect from someone who had never refereed more than the bantam game, and damn few at that. I knew with the crew that I had that there wouldn't be any problems, and my only concern was that I wouldn't let the guys down after the chance they had given me. As it turned out, I had no chance to fail. They worked as hard as they would have in any CFL game and they reminded me after the game that if you have a good crew, anyone can referee.

During the 1960s, Winnipeg was a hotbed of amateur football with teams reaching the national finals in a number of divisions. With the exception of junior football, officials didn't travel. Unless there was a final in your hometown you never got the chance to work a Canadian final. I was very fortunate working national finals in every division except college football, because the Vanier Cup was always played in Toronto.

The Queens and University of Manitoba Western Bowl final, which finished in overtime in the dark, was unquestionably the most exciting game I ever worked, but the results of most others remain a blur.

What remains vivid are situations where men, both players and officials, rise to the occasion to make the play or make the call, and yes, sometimes fail, but always get up again. Perhaps the most vivid memory I have of any playoff game happened in the Canadian Juvenile Final between Fort Garry and Montreal at the University of Manitoba. With only a minute remaining, Fort Garry lined up to kick a field goal that would provide the margin of victory—a miss, a Fort Garry loss.

The last thing officials want to do is decide the outcome of a game, particularly in a national championship. Bud Ulrich and I lined up under an upright and waited. Bang. The kick was up and heading high over Bud's post. As the ball sailed over his upright I knew by the look on his face that you needed a micrometer to determine whether it was good. No matter what he called, it was going to be wrong, and what made it worse, it would decide the national championship. What did he call? I can't remember, but I can remember the look on his face, and the reaction of both teams.

Like every official who has aspirations of working in the CFL, after years you wonder if the call is ever going to come. Experience is no longer an issue, you've done all playoffs at the national level, had good ratings, everyone said you're ready, so why don't they call?

It was 1969 and another year had passed. Still no call. But things were looking up: I had two pair of referee pants, I bought a car with brakes, the kids were out of diapers, and the family production line appeared to have taken a permanent rest.

While I was disappointed, I wasn't totally discouraged because I shared the same feeling with a dozen amateur officials in the West who all thought they deserved an opportunity to show they could do the job in the big-time. So life continued as usual, working five games a week while trying to figure out how to get the work done around the house, without much success.

In late September, with the season half over, the call finally came. "Neil, this is Andy Currie. Are you still interested in officiating in the CFL?"

I wanted to ask him to repeat the question but I knew the call was for real. Andy was the supervisor of Western officials but my first thought was, why is he calling me now, the training school for the CFL isn't until next year, but I quickly responded, "Yes, sir."

In a matter of fact voice he told me, "You'll work as the Field Judge in the Sunday afternoon game in Winnipeg," which in the 1960s meant I'd work on the line of scrimmage. He wished me luck and hung up.

The bad news was I hadn't received any CFL training, which I must admit in those days was limited. It was the middle of the season and I didn't know the crew. The good news was, I didn't have time to worry about the bad news. The next thing I knew I was sitting in the dressing room waiting, after nine years of apprenticeship, to step across that white line. I wish I could remember more about the game but I was in shock and can only recall a few incidents.

I've found out that the only reason I got the game was because a veteran official was suspended during the week and no other CFL official was available. It also looked like a safe game because Winnipeg was basically out of the playoffs. But that quickly changed when Winnipeg traded team favourite Dave Raimey for quarterback Wally Gabler from

Toronto in a last ditch bid to make the playoffs.

Prior to the game, I was reminded that, as with all CFL sideline officials, I was not allowed to bring a whistle on the field. If I wanted to kill a play, I simply put my arm in the air and one of the three officials in the centre of the field would blow their whistle. What they didn't say was they'd only blow it if they felt like it, or if they thought I was right. Sidemen were definitely considered second-class officials.

It didn't take long to find out how much I missed my whistle. Soon after the opening kickoff I was covering a ball carrier down the sideline when he stepped out of bounds. I quickly ran and marked the spot and put my arm in the air for a whistle. The silence was deafening. Either the other officials didn't see me or didn't care because I was a rookie. It didn't matter, I felt like a little school kid who put his arm up to leave the room, and was ignored by the teacher.

The trade had injected new life into the Bombers and we had a real battle on our hands. Late in the second quarter Gabler was intercepted, but he attempted to come upfield to make the tackle, which in those days meant almost certain death for the quarterback. The play was away from me so I covered Wally as he moved up field. Sure enough he got flattened by a Calgary blocker, but quickly got to his feet and smacked the Calgary player right in the mouth. In a split second my flag was in the air. How dare you punch someone in the face right in front of me, I thought. I grabbed veteran referee Taylor Patterson, who was working his last season and firmly suggested we throw the Winnipeg quarterback out of the game. He looked me in the eye and said, "There ain't no way we're throwing a quarterback out of the game. Besides, they can't hurt anyone."

He was probably right, but we would have been doing both Winnipeg and Wally a favour because they both ended up getting hammered. Still, I did get a chance to show everyone what an officious and precise official I could be.

Late in the game Winnipeg tight end Mitch Zalnasky (yes, there were tight ends in the CFL), whose running style more closely resembled that of a Clydesdale than a thoroughbred, and whose speed could only be matched by that same Clydesdale trying to pull a full load of beer up a steep incline, somehow managed to twist, stumble and miraculously bang his way 50 yards down to the Calgary goal line where he was finally tackled. Official Payne was right on the spot, marking

Mitch's incredible adventure two inches short of the goal line. My spot might have been correct but my judgment was lousy. The louder the crowd booed, the more emphatically I pointed to the spot. I'm not sure if I was trying to convince the crowd or myself that I was correct.

Poor Mitch; he never came that close to the goal line again, even in practice. In spite of my goal line antics, the film apparently confirmed that I did an adequate job. The end of the season was followed by a formal invitation to attend the spring school for the training of CFL officials. Yes!

3

Off to Boot Camp

The CFL's spring training schools, particularly those in the 1970s, were one of the highlights of the season, and in several respects haven't changed in 30 years. They have increased in length from two to four days, but still consist of officials putting in long grueling days on physical fitness, medical testing, mechanics, film work, and of course, the dreaded exams.

The days are long, with classes often running from seven in the morning until nine at night. But make no mistake, the effort expended during the days was equally matched by after-hour revelry, even if somewhat reduced in recent years because of the increased time and effort required for training as well as a more business-like approach by the league.

The most significant area of change has occurred in the training of officials. In the early '70s schools consisted of the officials locking themselves in a small room for two days equipped only with only their rule books. The two days consisted of 30 strong-willed, opinionated men going through a rule book page by page, word by word, rarely getting by a paragraph without heated arguments as to its meaning or application. There were no training films, no physical or medical testing or real mechanics for on-field coverage. Considering the lack of tools, it's surprising the officiating was as good as it was.

As a rookie I was warned by Abe Kovnats, "Don't listen, you'll only get confused." Obviously not all rookies got the same advice. I remember one particularly bad school. There was an intense rivalry between eastern and western officials, and to make matters worse, both were led by cigar smoking lawyers, Syd Bercov from the west and Joe Rockhi from the east. By the end of the day, the room was so filled with smoke you could barely make out Hap Shouldice, our director of officiating, who was now a beaten man, not only because of the smoke, but because all the screaming and yelling was the equivalent of sending an electric shock through his hearing aid.

I can't believe we didn't develop lung cancer, although the smoke did eventually control those who couldn't keep their mouths shut. I remember John Chase, a rookie from Montreal showing up for the Friday session full of confidence and ready to go. By Friday evening he had a confused look on his face, which by Saturday evening was replaced by a blank stare into space. He wrote the exam Sunday morning but we never saw him again. Obviously he had paid too much attention.

In the early years, one thing no one paid much attention to was our physical conditioning. Many officials, including veterans, were not in shape. As a first step we were required to obtain medicals from our doctors, which included our weight. In some cases the results were either altered, or some of the guys only had one foot on the scale.

The day of reckoning had arrived. We had just sat down for the Friday night session at the Skyline Hotel in Toronto, when Bill Fry, who had just joined the supervisory staff, stood up and barked: "Follow me."

We followed Bill single-file through the foyer of the hotel like a kindergarten class on a field trip; the only thing missing was the rope to hold on to.

As we headed to our unknown destination, there was more than a little complaining about being treated like kids, particularly by Jim Lysack, who had to be convinced that he shouldn't bop Bill on the nose. The journey didn't last long. We headed straight down a narrow hall toward the hotel pub, which Maury Mulhern, a veteran official from Vancouver, had discovered and explored earlier. I couldn't believe it! It was only Friday night and the league was going to buy us a beer.

But suddenly we made a sharp right-hand turn and ended up in the health club. Now Bill lined us up, and one-by-one made sure we had both feet on the scale as he carefully recorded our weight. Not surprisingly, there were a few red faces when some weights did not come close to those recorded on their medicals.

Other changes quickly followed. Bill Fry introduced comprehensive field mechanics, which changed officiating from ball watching to specific responsibilities for every official on every play. Now officials were assigned specific receivers to cover downfield as they crossed the line of scrimmage, or to cover the blocking or the ball carrier on a running play, but not both. Or they were simply assigned to watch the holding on either the right or left side of the line scrimmage, depending whether you were the referee or umpire.

With today's mechanics, if an official is doing his job there are many plays where he never sees the ball, unlike the old days where every official looked for the ball on every play and inevitably missed a linebacker knocking down a receiver as he tried to run a pass pattern, or a defensive back sticking his fingers in the slot back's eyes.

As with all aspects of society, evaluation of performance became an issue.

At one extreme was the less than adequate system of the 1970s, which consisted of being informed of a bad call in the men's room just before the next game. The only indirect notification you received on a satisfactory season was either a playoff game or invitation to the next year's school. Even without a basic system, officials who were honest with themselves knew when they were doing a good job. What was missing was identification and help in specific areas where improvement was required.

Don Barker, who succeeded Bill Fry as a director of officiating, introduced the first truly comprehensive evaluation of officials. Every game, officials are graded on conditioning, coverage, attitude, signals, application of the rules, and the most important component, judgment. With the advent of video technology, supervisors can grade officials on every play on what they did or didn't do. It doesn't take long for a pattern to emerge, where officiating behavior becomes predictable, particularly in pressure situations. Now officials not only have to deal with a scrutiny of television replay, the coaches, players, fans, and post-game dissection by the media, but most of all, the dreaded league video, the harshest critic of all. During the year, officials receive their own personal tapes showing their performance in the games they worked, which hopefully shows an even balance between the good and bad calls they have made.

In most instances, the tapes provide a positive review, with hopefully a nudge in the right direction where performance can be improved. However poor performances, to which no official is immune, vividly expose not only an official's weakness on the field but sometimes his own inadequacy in certain situations. To many officials, this additional evaluation of their performance is welcome and provides an opportunity to improve. To others it is just another level of criticism in a profession to a large extent built on criticism and abuse, which some find difficult if not impossible to handle. A sign reading "anyone with self doubt need not apply," should be hung over every official's dressing room door.

The infamous weigh-in ceremony also brought about immediate change in pre-season preparation requirements for officials. Our fitness expert had relayed the message loud and clear that mental performance was tied directly to physical conditioning, and that because of the stress of the job, officials who were not in shape were at risk on the field. The die had been cast. Officials were now required to report in shape to the school, which was now being held annually in Winnipeg. As in any group, not everyone passed the fitness test requirements, and some were forced to miss games until they got into shape, or retired.

In 1985, Larry Rohan, an excellent official from Vancouver and Washington who had worked on my crew, failed to meet the fitness standards. As a supervisor of the school and his friend, I had to give Larry the news. In my usual straightforward but less than tactful manner, I told Larry that he wasn't in shape and he would be at risk if we put him on the field.

Then, as a friend I told him to think of his family and get into better shape. Within the hour Larry was lying on the ground with a massive heart attack. It was off to Misericordia Hospital, where Larry would have the fight of his life. I contacted Ted Bartman, who at the time was both head of the hospital and president of the Blue Bombers. Frankly they didn't think Larry would make it.

The next day was one of the longest and most difficult of my life. I picked up Larry's wife, his three young kids and his brother at the airport. We headed for the hospital where Larry was hanging on by a thread. We spent the next 12 hours sitting in the waiting room afraid to breathe, while Larry's three kids played happily on the floor, oblivious to their dad's fight for life.

In spite of the massive damage, somehow Larry managed to survive. As an official on the field, Larry had the personality we all would have died for. Pressure never bothered him and I'm sure his heart rate was no different whether he was doing a playoff game or playing with his kids in the park. I'm certain that Larry's ability to stay cool and relax under pressure was a major factor in saving his life, even when the doctors didn't give him much of a chance.

While Larry was out of danger, he wasn't well enough to travel, and spent the next several weeks as our houseguest. On more than one occasion I couldn't help feel that it was his way of getting even for the fitness test I put him through.

Larry was not only an American but also a Vietnam veteran. What a lethal combination. Our crew used to take turns rooming with Larry on the road listening to his war stories, some of which may actually have been true. I can't remember how many times I heard about cows being pushed out of helicopters, but it beat counting sheep those sleepless nights on the road. Larry's revenge was now complete. Our family was a prisoner in its own home, sharing the stories I had heard a hundred times before from this lovable but typical transplanted American, who I was still fortunate enough to have as a friend.

I was continually amazed by the socializing and partying that lasted into the wee hours of the morning at our annual school, particularly after 10 to 12 hours in the classroom and the prospect of an exam early the next morning, which could decide your future in the league.

If you walked through the hotel you were bound to find a group of officials clutching their glasses arguing about what would be on the exam the next morning, an interpretation of some obscure rule, or down in the local pub with one of the guys up on the stage, giving Diamond Lil a hand.

There was also a lot of talent at the supervisory level. In 1986, Don Barker and I got to the finals of the comedy contest at the Château Lacombe in Edmonton, but got beat in the end by a woman who was blessed with gigantic breasts. For the first couple of years I thought these escapades were nothing more than the boys getting together to have a few drinks to blow off some steam. I didn't realize it was a ritual that had been going on for years, as necessary as a salmon swimming upstream to spawn.

With all due respect to the great armies of the world, the officials' school had all the elements of an army getting ready for war. We had our three days of basic training, and many of us would not see each other again for a long time as we worked on different crews; or perhaps never again, because inevitably some would fail to make it back for the next year.

For many, it would be the last time they would completely relax until the season was over. Rules of conduct changed dramatically. No drinking after you leave your home for the game, let alone being seen in any place where liquor is served. And yes, keep your mouth shut, only rank and serial number were to be provided to the enemy. Coaches and players who you joked with in the off-season were now deadly serious about winning; their livelihood depended on it, and they took no prisoners.

The school wound up Sunday afternoon with firm handshakes, hugs and good luck wishes as everyone scattered across the country, knowing full well what they would face for the next six months, and that the only people you could depend on were those you just spent the last three days with.

Every school produced its own tales. If you were looking for entertainment, Don Barker, after much coaxing and several drinks, would do his Cassius Clay imitation, which because of its popularity and longevity was updated to include the Mohammed Ali years. If you liked fairy tales, without any encouragement Bill Hagans would tell you why the Maple Leafs would win the Stanley Cup although inevitably they were off to the golf course before the playoffs began.

We took turns falling in love with the bar singer. One year, Bud Ulrich was smitten by a gorgeous blond singer. When he returned to his room he hoped to include her in his dreams. Better yet, the guys had removed her full-sized model from the lobby, and she was waiting for Bud in bed when he got there. His eyes were like saucers when he turned on the lights.

Most of my memories involved Ross Perrier, because Bill Fry insisted Ross and I room together, reasoning that only two officials instead of four would get in trouble if he separated us. Our room was always party headquarters and I remember one night an uninvited female guest wandered into our room and passed out in the bathtub full of beer and ice. Not wanting to embarrass either her or ourselves, Jim Lysak threw his size 46 jacket over our guest to keep her warm, making it extra difficult to find the beer.

Undoubtedly the most memorable school was held in 1970 in Gimli, Manitoba, a small Icelandic fishing town located 60 miles north of Winnipeg. It marked the first time that eastern and western officials ever attended the same school. Other than a mixed crew of officials at the Grey Cup, there was absolutely no contact between the two sets of officials. Andy Currie, the western supervisor of officials, was also a senior executive at the City of Winnipeg, and got a deal on the city transit bus to transport the officials to Gimli. It must have been a good price because the shocks and springs had long since been removed.

The out-of-town officials were picked up at the Winnipeg airport and we headed north for Gimli. In 1970 the airlines were still serving free liquor, and where there were freebees you could count on officials being at the head of the line, right behind the media.

It didn't take long before the spring-less and shock-less bus had done its job on the rough Manitoba roads. Moaning and groaning was replaced by pleas from the filled-to-capacity Air Canada kidneys to "please stop the bus." Andy Currie, who I believe was a Scottish Presbyterian (and if he wasn't he should have been) because of his no-nonsense, shoulder to the wheel attitude, continued in silence to ignore everyone's pleas, although his countenance turned redder and more agitated with each painful mile.

Finally, from the back of the bus, a voice clearly in the last stages of desperation blurted out, "If you don't stop this damn bus, I'll pee on the floor." As the bus came to a stop, a handful of its western occupants all tried to exit simultaneously through the same door. After what seemed an eternity, they all silently clambered back onto the bus looking much relieved for their experience.

Andy was not impressed. But neither were the eastern officials when we pulled into Gimli. Our home for the weekend was a converted World War II Air Force training centre, and I'm sure that I use that term generously, because it appeared more suited for a survival course than a football clinic.

The shots from our visiting eastern brothers were unrelenting. Prior to the school, eastern officials thought the only thing their western brothers were good for was drinking, which they had now confirmed. Western officials, however, did not hold their eastern counterparts in such high regard.

When we disembarked we were provided with a bed roll that would hopefully cover one of the many steel beds that were in the dormitories scattered throughout the compound, as well as a stern warning to watch out for bear traps. What they didn't tell us was the camp was pitch black at night and if we ran into a bear or trap it was too late.

As it turned out, we didn't have time to worry about bears because we were too busy dodging the skunks that were living under the dorms. If nothing else, the spartan conditions brought the eastern and western officials closer together, and by the time the Saturday session was over the only obvious difference was that eastern officials wore their flags in the front and the western officials in the back.

Combining eastern and western officials in the same school was probably the largest single factor in making officiating more consistent between both ends of the country. Part of Andy's plan in choosing Gimili was to isolate us and keep us out of trouble, but after a long but successful Saturday, the boys were ready for a little relaxation. But where?

Andy hadn't counted on Maury Mulhern, who was also a successful hotelier and could pinpoint any hotel pub within 10 miles. In an effort to promote unity between east and west, a Western delegation invited Bill Dell, a non-drinking eastern referee, to join them in their search for the Holy Grail. It didn't take long before Maury located a rustic fisherman's pub that had remained unchanged over the century. Bill was living proof that you didn't have to drink to have fun and was quickly adopted by his western brothers.

However when the beer was ordered and covered the entire table, Bill's inexperience began to show when he questioned, "Why would you order beer for the whole night all it once?" Almost immediately all the suds disappeared and the question was answered, although someone feebly explained that it was to avoid waiting if the waiter was busy.

As the 'happy gang' made its way back to camp, it may have been pitch black, but it was far from silent. Small groups had gathered, glasses in hand, to solve all problems of football officiating, or making new friends from the other end of the country.

The success of the school had obviously relieved some of the pressure Andy felt in attempting to bring stubborn strongly opinioned men together. He had decided to join us in a drink, which he did only on special occasions. To ensure Scotch was available, he brought his own supply and poured himself a generous drink, which he uncharacteristically followed with another, obviously enjoying both the evening and the company. It wasn't long before Andy realized his obligation not to get too close to the troops. He excused himself and dutifully, but not steadily, disappeared into the darkness in search of his cabin.

Sunday morning soon arrived, along with the dreaded exam, made more excruciating by Andy, who was a former teacher, always insisting on precise and detailed answers. Andy's rigid and inflexible demands inevitably brought bitter protests from all the officials, who after the previous night's activities were no match for the master. As we waited in our seats for Andy to arrive with the exam, it was obvious that, as usual, some of the officials were under the weather, no doubt as a result of the breeze off Lake Winnipeg.

As Andy walked into the room, exams under arm, it was hard to ignore his rather large black eye, which he had acquired the night before in a losing battle with a large oak tree in that darkened search for his cabin. It was the one and only time we started out even on a Sunday morning.

4

Hey, Rookie

The day of reckoning was fast approaching; my first season in the CFL. Eight years of amateur officiating, numerous clinics and examinations, and Canadian finals were all behind me. It was time to deliver.

My first game was Calgary at Edmonton, two teams that have genuinely hated each other for the last 30 years. What a way to start. My emotions that last week before the game oscillated between "I can hardly wait," to "I sure hope I can do the job," and they changed as quickly as the Winnipeg weather.

Major championships usually end with a close-up shot of the hero hugging his parents and thanking them for all their support. Here I am, 31 years old and my mother and father are driving me to the airport, and to add to the embarrassment, they come inside and tell Abe Kovnats, who I'm working with in Edmonton, to look after their little boy. Little did I know it was a job he would take seriously in my rookie year, although on more than one occasion his help almost got us both fired.

My dad was a sports fanatic and on Grey Cup day we would lock the doors of the house and take the phone off hook to ensure we wouldn't be disturbed while we were watching the game. He was the only man I knew who could hold his breath for three hours, living and dying with every play. Not surprisingly, he was extremely proud when I was hired to work in the CFL, but never fully understood why they would hire his dopey son.

Our flight to Edmonton was also my first plane ride. Earlier, I had vowed never to climb onto an airplane until it was to do my first pro game. Thank God that date finally arrived, because I thought I was going to spend the rest of my life on trains and buses. I could even visualize driving to Disneyland with the four kids jammed in the back seat of our Austin.

As the plane touched down in Edmonton my stomach began to churn, knowing the game was only hours away. After the long trip from the Edmonton airport, which is located closer to Calgary than Edmonton, we arrived at our hotel and began packing our equipment for the game.

It didn't take long to face my first test, "Hey, rookie, ice the beer." It was a task I joyfully carried out in my rookie season, which also required great skill if the beer was to meet the temperature sensitive demands of thirsty officials, some five hours later after the game. It was a ritual I carried out 25 years later, when I came out of retirement to referee during the time of U.S. expansion.

After the usual pre-game meal, which for me consisted of tomato soup, which I was only able to swallow after considerable chewing, we headed for the stadium. My stomach was getting worse, but I was certain I would be all right once the whistle blew.

As we entered Clarke Stadium we were greeted by the overpowering smell of onions, which were being cooked for the game. The smell permeated every square inch of the stadium, and I'm sure it was permanently embedded in the concrete walls. My stomach had enough, and I quickly headed for the officials dressing room, dodging the laughs from the rest of the crew, hoping for some relief. As I opened the door I was greeted by a mound of hot dogs and an appropriate amount of onions, which were left for the officials. I spent the next hour sitting on the white throne with cold sweat running down my cheeks.

My new residence seemed like a wise move, because I remembered Ron Latourelle, the punt return specialist for the Bombers in the '50s and '60s, who still holds two Grey Cup records for punt returns, telling me about his first game as a Bomber and a pro.

It was late in the game when Bud Grant sent him in for the first time to return a punt, which he had to field in his own end zone. Ron said, "I was so scared I actually pooped my pants while I was standing waiting for the kick." After an hour on the throne I knew it wasn't something I'd have to worry about, but I knew exactly how he felt.

I now faced my second test. The referee's shoes were deposited at my feet with instructions to do a good job. I was a rookie but there was no way I was going to shine anyone's shoes. Cautiously I returned the shoes and suggested the referee could do a better job. Everyone laughed. Apparently I had passed the second test.

Finally, we were dressed. The joking and horseplay were replaced with a tense silence as we sat facing each other, some looking at the floor, others straight ahead, each getting ready in his own way for the night's work. Suddenly there were five long shrill warnings from the dressing room buzzer; five minutes to show time. It was a sound I had heard a hundred times before working the yardsticks at the Bomber games, but my stomach told me that this time it was different. I was now part of the main attraction on centre stage.

The rush of adrenaline I experienced as the crew jogged from the dressing room to the sideline was identical to that I experienced some eight years earlier on my first game on the Bomber yardsticks, which had driven me to become a CFL official. The stadium was packed, a regular occurrence for all CFL stadiums in the 1970s. The blue and gold colours which I had previously experienced, were replaced by a sea of green and gold, with a great number of fans also wearing hard hats, which accurately reflected the attitude of both the team and their fans.

I tried to calm my nerves by singing the anthem, but soon realized nothing was coming out, and in my present state, blowing my whistle would have defied the law of physics. I desperately grabbed a couple of pieces of ice off the Edmonton bench and popped them into my mouth on the way to my position for the opening kickoff.

My feelings on the opening kickoff were everything I expected. But I soon learned as a sideline official you're too damn busy to think about it, never mind enjoy it.

My stomach had stopped jumping but I was still nervous. Why I don't know, because I didn't have time to think. On every play it was count the offense, put up your arms for substitution, check the end, watch for procedure, tell the defensive end to move back, watch the slot in motion, keep your eye on the guard and tackle, listen to the coach screaming about offsides—all before the ball was actually snapped.

The speed and quickness of the players is incredible. Unlike amateur ball, where plays and situations develop, pro ball situations explode in a split second. If you lose your concentration for a moment, or you are in the wrong position, you're dead. I would soon learn that the remarkable speed of the game and the associated pressures and scrutiny of pro sports would make the jump from college to pro officiating more difficult than ever.

But, hey, I couldn't believe it, we were already late in the second quarter and everything was going well, and I had even made a couple of calls. The job wasn't that tough after all. On a first down play, Edmonton ran a sweep to my side, directly in front of their bench. The ball carrier was tackled. I was ready to blow my whistle. What happened? The ball was on the ground with half a dozen players trying to jump on it with everything happening right against the sideline. Finally the ball squirts out from underneath the pile and out of bounds.

Who touched it last? Thankfully I was in perfect position and saw the Calgary player touch the ball just before it hit the sideline. I quickly turn and signal Calgary ball. In a split second, the Edmonton bench was all over me. "Hey, rookie, you blew that one. Rookie enjoy the game, it's going to be your last. Edmonton touched the ball last you blind @#$&@*$&!"

Welcome to the CFL. It was an initiation every rookie official had to survive, and it was usually repeated on a regular basis, sometimes lasting several years.

I then broke the first cardinal rule of officiating. Don't think about your last call, move on to the next play, which sometimes can be difficult, whether you're a veteran or a rookie.

As Calgary lined up for the next play, the TV slow motion replay upstairs had shown I was absolutely right on what turned out to be a difficult call. But the Edmonton bench had done its job. They made me think about the call. Finally, I turned my attention to the next play and even though the ball hadn't been snapped, I was too late. I didn't have time to check all of my responsibilities, but thankfully I saw that Calgary did not have a properly numbered end, the number looked like a 66 instead of the required number in the 1970s. I quickly threw my flag for illegal procedure as the ball was snapped. I was glad I had flagged the play because Calgary gained 30 yards on the play.

At the end of the next play Herman Harrison, Calgary's outstanding tight end who wore No. 76, approached me like he had a secret and quietly told me, "Ref, I was the end on the play when you called that penalty."

He couldn't have done anymore damage if he kicked me between the legs with his size-twelve cleats. I had just broken rule number two, don't call a penalty unless you're absolutely sure. If you think it's a penalty, it might be a penalty, you're pretty sure it's a penalty, you saw most of the action and think it's a penalty, then guaranteed it's not a penalty.

I was still thinking about the fumble on the previous play and wasn't sure of the number at the end of a line, and I got caught.

Coaches will accept, albeit with great difficulty, an explanation as to why fouls are missed because officials can't see everything, but there is absolutely no rationale for calling nonexistent penalties. As we made our way to the dressing room for half-time I was disgusted with myself for making a bone-headed call when I wasn't absolutely sure, something I could not remember doing in all my years as an amateur. What I didn't realize was that it was largely the pressure of my first game that was responsible for my mistake, and unfortunately people under pressure often do stupid or irrational things. I would soon learn that the ability to act under pressure separated the good from the bad officials.

As I sat in the dressing room, I was convinced that TV had shown everyone in the free world what a lousy call I had made, although at that point only Herman Harrison and I knew for sure. I was convinced that my eight years of hard work were down the drain. I now have some empathy for young pro golfers trying to make it to the PGA Tour who miss a short putt during the final stages of qualifying. Although, unlike me, they will get a chance to come back the following year and try again. Somehow I managed to get through the second half, but I knew the day of judgment would soon arrive.

Two days later I was in the Winnipeg dressing room wishing the crew good luck prior to their game, when Andy Currie made his inevitable appearance. "Neil, I'd like to talk to you," he said as he motioned me into the men's room. "It's about a play in the Edmonton game, a procedure call you made for no end."

Before I could come clean he continued, "What side of the field were you on?"

When I told him the Edmonton side, he looked puzzled. "That's strange. There was no end on the play, but on the other side of the field."

I had gotten lucky. There was no end on George Eakin's side, which he missed or decided not to call. Andy mumbled something about having the film in backwards, but I never heard another word. I wonder if George ever got hell for not making the call.

When I entered the men's room, I had expected to exit as a civilian. It would have been impossible to imagine that 20 years later I would be conducting the same interviews in the same washrooms. Later, when the area municipalities amalgamated into the city of Winnipeg, I acquired a new office. When I opened the closet, I found a projector and screen used by Andy to evaluate game films. I had inherited Andy's office.

But it was off to Regina for a Sunday afternoon game. The pregame requirements of the 1970s were pretty basic: show up for the game on time, be sober and make sure your uniform is pressed. Today officials are required to report the night before for a day game, or at least seven hours prior to a night game, leaving enough time to review films, relax and think about the game, with all of your travel and hotel arrangements looked after by the league.

Officials pay scales of the 1970s were very low, which we tried to supplement by saving money on our expenses. As a result, our hotels had to meet two criteria: they had to be cheap and accommodate as many men as possible in one room. If the CFL officials moved into your hotel, it was a sure sign that the wrecking ball or foreclosure weren't far behind. In the space of two years, we closed the Devonshire Hotel and the Georgian Towers in Vancouver and the Caravan Hotel in Calgary.

We no longer stay at the Drake Hotel in Regina, even though it is still standing. One Saturday night Tom Cheney, an official from Calgary, and I checked into the Drake for a Sunday afternoon game. We had just turned in when there was a raucous noise in the hall, including a loud thump on our door. I jumped out of bed to see what was happening but was quickly stopped by Tom, who yelled, "Payne you're not opening that door until tomorrow morning." The next morning I found a knife sticking in the outside of our door. Someone had either used the knife to open a can of red paint, or there was blood on the handle. It was time to move.

But at least we had a door on our room. Don Barker was scheduled to work a game in Montreal and was booked into the Mount Royal Hotel, a hotel whose very name suggested elegance and royalty. Don arrived late at night and it was obvious that the Royal was a tired old lady. After his five-hour flight from Vancouver, Don was tired and needed a good night's sleep before the next day's game. He quickly headed for his room.

He closed the door, but noticed there was no lock on it. Adding further to the problem the door wouldn't stay closed. Back to the front desk, where he demanded another room. The front desk clerk was quick to point out to Don that he was fortunate to have a door, as most of the other doors had been removed by the demolition crew. It was too late to change hotels so Don spent the rest of the night with a chair propped up against the door, trying to sleep with one eye open, which isn't a bad exercise for a referee who has to keep one eye on the quarterback and the other on the holding infractions of the offensive line.

We stayed at the Mayfair Hotel in Edmonton, which at the time was quite run down, but was later refurbished. We knew we were in the right hotel when we got picked up at the airport by the airport limo. The driver asked where we were going. "To the Mayfair," we said.

"You must be CFL officials," he observed.

Again, instant recognition. But we couldn't resist asking, "How did you know?"

"You're the only ones who stay there anymore," he said. We knew exactly what he meant.

Hap Shouldice came west to Edmonton to supervise one of our games and spent his one and only night at the Mayfair. After our post-game meeting, we returned to our rooms and turned in. It wasn't long before the fire alarm went off, and we all scrambled down to the lobby, passing the fireman on their way up. But where was Hap? We called his room but there was no answer. He had taken his hearing aid out for the night, and was enjoying a hot bath.

We scrambled back up the stairs, and dragged a soaking wet director of officiating back downstairs, where we were joined in the lobby by the most unsavory looking group of half clad hotel guests.

The next day Hap flew to Calgary to take in the last game in his western swing. When Hap got into the cab at the airport, he asked the driver to take him to the Caravan. The driver gave Hap a quizzical look but followed the theory that the customer is always right.

When they got to the Caravan, Hap paid the driver, grabbed his bag and got out of the cab. It was his first trip to the Calgary hotel, but it didn't take long for him to realize that he stood in front of a pile of rubble that was once the Caravan. Hap had seen enough and soon after the league was looking after our hotel arrangements.

My next several games went reasonably well and I seemed to be getting better, but officiating was consuming a great deal of nervous energy. I spent two days after each game going over every play, identifying what I could have done better, then three days preparing for the next game, becoming increasingly nervous as game day approached.

For the first time Gloria was beginning to question whether it was worth it. "I don't mind you being away for games, but even when you're here, you might as well be somewhere else, because you're out in space a million miles away." She was right; something had to change. Perhaps I couldn't handle the pressure of pro ball, and should give it up.

My next game was in Calgary, and I knew things wouldn't get any better because I was getting to work my first game with Paul Dojack, undoubtedly the best-known and most respected CFL referee of all time. To add to the pressure, I was also going to be Paul's roommate.

Paul had already checked in to the Caravan, a hotel already doomed by our presence, when I approached the door of our room on an incredibly hot August afternoon. The curtains on the windows were pulled, so I knew Paul, who was getting close to retirement, was lying down trying to get some rest before the game. I knocked quietly on the door. After repeated attempts, I heard Paul trying to open the door to the blackened room. When it swung open, he stood in a pair of long white underwear. As quickly as he greeted me with a warm and friendly welcome, he turned and bounced back into bed, pulling the covers up to his chin, while I stood still sweating from the heat of the Calgary day. I couldn't help think that if his underwear were green he could have a career playing a leprechaun in Irish movies.

There I was, a rookie rooming with the greatest of them all, who was just as nervous as I was. I was no longer worried about being nervous, and thankfully, after a continuing battle and growing confidence, I was generally able to confine the problem to the pre-game shakes.

The year 1970 also marked the officials' last stand in trying to maintain control of television, which brought essential revenues to the CFL. Control of the game had traditionally been the officials divine right, and change was not easily accepted. A clandestine procedure was developed where officials and the TV networks would take on-field timeouts for commercials in such a manner that the fans in the stands wouldn't notice. The system was so successful that not only did the fans not notice, but most of the time, neither television nor the officials knew they were in commercial.

The system was designed for failure. It had been set up so that officials were responsible for the exact play when a time-out was to be taken, with television dictating the general time in which a commercial break was required. As a sideline official my job was to coordinate the time out between the referee and the television people, who were located at centre field at the timer's table, just off the sideline.

The typical scenario involved the referee telling me, "After the next play we'll take the time out." I would then sprint 60 yards to the timer's bench with my tongue hanging out to tell the TV producer to take a time-out, and wait there until it was over, only to turn and see the referee had forgotten, and was running the next play. This was the signal for the TV people to start screaming at me, "Stop the play!" It was back on my horse with tongue dragging on the field, apologetically telling the referee he missed a time-out.

Hell, I was only a rookie so why not shoot the messenger. "I meant the next play," he barked with a look that made me feel like a mental incompetent, and told me to return to the timer's bench to again inform the TV people. I could hardly wait to get back to the timer's bench, where the TV people were going crazy because we ran a play during the time-out. "Guess what guys, the referee has just taken the TV time-out."

I still remember the producer damn near choking himself with the cord from his headset as he jumped out of his chair to try and get at me. "We just finished our time-out, tell that (censored) referee to start the game." Meanwhile, the announcers upstairs in the booth stumbled around trying to think of something to say while the officials and players stood around.

Once again, back to the referee, my speed now reduced to a slow jog, partly because of the onset of exhaustion, partly because I knew the referee wasn't going to be any happier than the TV people had been. "Paul, the TV people said they've already got their time-out and they want you to start the game right away."

The response was no surprise. "Who do they think they are, we're running the game and we'll tell them when to take a time-out." So we would take every last second of the time-out, which had now become an eternity for the announcers in the TV booth. This scenario continued throughout the year, with both television and game officials sharing the blame. Although more often than not, it was the officials' insistence on maintaining control of every aspect of the game that precipitated the problem.

By the end of the season, the TV producers despised me more than the coaches. Hell, the poor coaches never got their chance to scream and yell at me because I was too busy running to the timer's table for the time-outs. Regrettably, they would all eventually get their turn, even if it took an extra year or two.

The television dollars were too important, so the Keystone Cop acts were soon eliminated. Television took over total control for starting and stopping the game for all of its commercials. In reality, it was the only way to go, and removed an onerous responsibility from the referee that had nothing to do with the game itself.

My continuing trips between plays to the timer's table for TV commercials was a great conditioning program, but made concentrating on the real job even more difficult. I had been warned numerous times that as a rookie I would be constantly challenged by the players and coaches, who were looking for that little edge that might make the difference between winning and losing. There were also some coaches who genuinely hated officials, and considered it their moral obligation, handed down from George Halas, the grandfather of professional football, to try and harass and intimidate any official within hailing distance.

While players presented a different problem, rarely was their conduct on the field a concern. They either recognized that, like themselves, our jobs were just as difficult, and on occasion when they did explode, it was over quickly because their concentration was required for the next play. In all my years, I can't recall more than a couple of occasions where I had to flag players for their conduct, although there probably should have been a few more. But any official worth his salt tries to avoid this type of call, and will only resort to the flag when he is being publicly embarrassed, or the player's actions bring the integrity of the game into question.

I can't remember how many times I walked beside a player listening to his less than complementary description of some of the qualities of my officiating, but there was never any thought of flag because only he and I knew what he was saying. It wasn't uncommon for that same player, several plays later, to return and apologize for what happened in the heat of the battle.

Of greater concern was the fact that players were always looking for the edge that would help beat the man they were facing on the other side of the line. It was the defensive end lining up just a little offside, so the tackle couldn't block him on his way to the quarterback;

or the same tackle holding just long enough so he wouldn't get called and the end wouldn't get to the quarterback on time; or the slot back trying to hit the line of scrimmage at full tilt as the ball was being snapped to get a jump on the defensive back, who was trying to grab his sweater just long enough so the ball was overthrown; or a player simply whacking the hell out of an opponent trying to intimidate him to gain control.

As a rookie I was tested many times and my education as a pro official had only just begun. Being a sideline official in the CFL, with all this motion, was difficult enough without the players trying to see how far they could push you.

One of my first experiences was with Terry Evanshen, the wide receiver with the Calgary Stampeders. Terry looked more like a jockey, but what a player. He was rightfully elected into the Hall of Fame in 1984 after a life-threatening and debilitating car accident.

In the first quarter, he lined up on my side and dutifully ran his pass patterns after the ball was snapped. No problem, it gave me time to pay attention to the defensive line. Suddenly, he was off the line of scrimmage like he was shot out of a cannon and quickly grabbed the pass for a long gain. That little fart, I thought. Not only did he beat the defensive back, I think he beat me as well. He was offside.

There was no way I would let that happen again. I watched Terry like a hawk, play after play, without seeing anything. Then, bang, he did it again. But I didn't go for my flag because it was so quick. Sure enough, he did it several more times but it was too late to call. I had set the standard and had to live with it.

I knew Andy Currie would review the game films, so I beat him to the punch and asked him to look at the plays where I thought I was beaten. It didn't take long. The phone rang the next day. "Neil, it's Andy." I braced for the worst. "You're right, Evanshen was offside on one or two plays." I began to wonder whether I had the guts to make the call as Andy continued, "but I had to run the projector in slow motion several times to see it."

In reality, Terry had pushed the rules to their absolute limit and thankfully I hadn't reacted with an unnecessary penalty. I was making the adjustment to officiating at the pro level and didn't even know it. As a supervisor, I would later learn that no official can be criticized for a split second judgment made on the field, which can only be confirmed with repeated slow motion replays, a luxury he didn't have when he made the call.

As luck would have it, I had Montreal again for my next game. The script didn't change with Evanshen driving Payne crazy with his quick getaways off a line, inevitably catching a pass when he seemed to get that extra jump. But still no flag. Then it happened. Before I could think, like a western gunslinger, my flag was out of my pocket and on the ground. He had stepped over the line. Not only had I set the standard for the player, but more importantly, for myself.

The rest of the season had its many ups as downs, as I was still trying to prove to myself and to my peers that I really belonged. My next game was my first visit to Empire Stadium and the B.C. Lions. It was the perfect opportunity to make my mark. Jim Young, the Lions' slot back and another Hall of Famer, would line up on my side. Jim was universally known as "Dirty 30," for his alleged dirty tactics. I say alleged, because he had never been caught by an official, although coaches and general managers bitterly complained about the beating he administered to their defensive backs. Veteran officials were convinced Jim studied the positioning of officials on film and knew the areas we couldn't cover.

We arrived at the Stadium two hours before game time and took a tour around the field on a gorgeous Vancouver evening. Jim had already arrived and was sitting alone in the stands in a virtually empty stadium, already half dressed and getting psyched for the game.

Little does he know, I thought, but this was the night he would get caught. I was determined to watch him from the time he left the huddle until he got back to his bench. He didn't have a chance. In our five-men coverage, the sideman and I didn't really have any formal responsibility after the ball was snapped other than covering the ball and a lot of sidemen never looked downfield because they might have to make a pass interference call, and that was the area where all the problems were occurring.

Play after play, I diligently covered No. 30 downfield and back to the huddle with absolutely nothing happening, although the defensive back covering Young must have shared my concerns because every time Jim got close to the defender he looked like he was on hot coals. The first half passed without incident and I was beginning to think that the "Dirty 30" reputation was, in fact, exaggerated. Early in the third quarter

B.C. was intercepted and I ended up covering the ball carrier down my sideline. I marked the out of bounds, but before I could look up someone was yelling incoherently in my ear. It was the defensive back who had now taken his hand away from his blood-covered mouth, pointing to what appeared to be less than a full set of teeth, screaming about being elbowed in the mouth by "Dirty 30." I quickly looked for No. 30, who was now heading for his bench on the far side of the field, but he stopped at a safe distance to survey the damage he had created. Mission accomplished. For the rest of the game, "Dirty 30" was free to run his pass patterns at will, and ended up catching several long passes.

For the next several seasons I watched Mr. Young, but with less and less enthusiasm because I began to believe no one would ever catch him, and I knew if I continued to watch him I'd miss something far more important.

Probably the most difficult job for a rookie sideline official was trying to keep the defensive line one yard away from the ball. Each team had at least one defensive lineman who would continue to get closer and closer. If you didn't penalize him, he would eventually own both you and the line of scrimmage. Establishing a yard was made more difficult by the lack of any real standard. In fact there were three shifting standards, one for ordinary scrimmage plays, one for third down short yardage, and one for goal line situations where the helmets of the offensive and defensive lines had to darn near touch before there was a flag.

My first lesson came early, with Junior Ah You, a defensive end with the Alouettes, who relied on his quickness. Like other Hall of Famers he had that uncanny ability to drive officials crazy. On the first play of the game he lined up on my side, and looked over towards me on the sideline to confirm that he was lined up onside. I nodded. No problem, he was well back. I thought, man this is a great player, concerned about being onside. The next play, he lined up just offside and didn't bother looking toward me on the sideline. I concluded that it was just poor judgment on his part.

The next play he lined up again in the same spot. After the play I caught his attention. "No. 72, you're close to being offside. Move back." I had long since learned that you didn't tell a player he was offside on the previous play because of the inevitable response: "If I was offside, why the hell didn't you call it?" to which there is no logical response.

Sure enough, on the next play he was back in the same place. If I don't call this one, I thought, I might as well take my whistle and go home. I let the flag fly. Again on the next play he was back in the same place, still offside. Now both of us are asking the same question. Will I throw another flag and try to maintain a consistent standard, or give in to his crowding the line of scrimmage? The ball is snapped and out comes the flag for a second time. Before the flag hit the ground, the Montreal bench was all over me. They knew I was a rookie and were doing their best to intimidate me.

What do I do if he lines up in the same place again on the next play? Thankfully, he didn't want to risk it, and lined up onside where he belonged. While the battle was over, the war wasn't. With every official in every game it's a never-ending fight to keep the players onside while trying to minimize the number of flags, which no one likes to see.

The one yard the defense had to be off the ball, or lack thereof, used to drive some coaches wacky, and rightly so, because whatever a yard meant it wasn't 36 inches, and it rapidly shrunk in short yardage situations.

In the 14 years that Ray Jauch was a head coach in the CFL, the only thing he ever complained about was the defensive yard. It drove him crazy. Coach Jauch could not understand how a yard could be anything else than the required 36 inches, which made him a perfect candidate for teaching math at Massachusetts Institute of Technology, but a potential basket case for coaching in the CFL. Every pre-game meeting with Coach Jauch was educational, defining the exact length of a yard accompanied by his pleas to enforce the standard rigidly, all from an extremely competitive and frustrated coach whose truly gentlemanly qualities never permitted him to raise the rhetoric above "golly gee," even though he probably wanted to wring our necks.

To his credit, he did very little complaining during the game, letting the officials concentrate on their jobs, with the exception of the odd impassioned outburst where obvious offsides appeared to be ignored.

It appeared that a reconciliation between Coach Jauch's and the officials' standard for offside was impossible, but as a land surveyor in my other life, I thought I had the solution. I cut six inches off a wooden yardstick I had at home, and reattached the pieces with a hinge so that fully extended the yardstick was still 36 inches. You also could fold the short piece underneath and it would measure 30 inches. I presented the yardstick to Coach Jauch fully extended, explaining he could use it around the house in the normal manner. I then reduced yardstick to 30 inches and told him that this was the yardstick used to measure a yard in the CFL. I'm not sure that he was overly impressed, as his competitive nature would never let go, but our future discussions on the properties of a yard seemed much lighter and far more understanding.

The job done by the sideline officials of the CFL is a great challenge, particularly when the motion of the game is factored in. In my early games as a supervisor, sitting in the comfort and safety of my booth, I'd see a linebacker bust up the middle, or slot back hit the line of scrimmage, both of whom clearly appeared offside.

I could hardly wait to get downstairs after the game and give the officials hell for missing the call. The next day I would review the calls on film and find out that I was wrong. The linebacker had been extremely quick and his timing was perfect and he wasn't offside. The story with the slot back was the same. By Wednesday I was phoning the same officials I criticized on Sunday telling them that I was wrong, which again only confirms that unless you see the entire action you will be wrong if you try to make a call. The accuracy of the sideman's decisions is even more remarkable when you consider the ten or twelve judgments that he is required to make on every play.

But the officials are far from being alone with their decisions. Every move they make is closely watched and energetically commented on by the league's passionate, stubborn and always foxy CFL coaches.

5

What Did You Say, Coach?

Dealing with individual coaches is one of an official's greatest challenges. From December to June, CFL coaches are generally mild-mannered citizens. They could very well go unnoticed as your next-door neighbour, taking out the garbage, shoveling the walk, driving their kids to an early morning hockey game at the local arena.

Sunday afternoons in football season these ordinary men are suddenly transformed into surly paranoids or raving lunatics and just about everything in between. I've known only a handful who managed to stay completely cool.

Their collective psychosis is understandable and even predictable when you consider that all week, offensive and defensive game plans are prepared with precision and detail that would make General Patton look like a private. Come the Sunday afternoon, coaches are forced to stand on the sideline in front of the whole nation to watch their futures being decided by 12 players, who at best are young boys disguised in men's bodies, over whom the coach has no control once they have crossed the white line. If by some chance the players actually execute his game plan, the coach still has one final hurdle to clear: the officials.

To coaches, officials at their best are inconsistent and at their worst, incompetent. No doubt there has been more than one official's call that has been the final straw that sends a coach to the unemployment line.

There isn't one official who has patrolled the sidelines in the CFL who hasn't been reminded by more than one coach after a call he didn't like that: "You're taking the food out of my kids' mouths... That call could cost me my job."

I can think of no other job that is more dependent on the actions of other people, many of which are either the officials' split second judgments or the execution of a play by the players. And the results are as often from good luck as they are from good planning. So the next time you see the coach lose it on the sideline, more often than not it's his way of dealing with events over which he has no control.

A university degree in psychology would have been far more beneficial than attending officiating school in learning to deal with head coaches. One of my earlier and regular encounters was with Bud Riley, head coach of the Blue Bombers from 1972 to 1974. It didn't take long before I felt Bud's presence behind me on the sideline. His language was educational, but his description of my body parts and sexual activities, while very vivid, were less than flattering. But after a few games I noted something peculiar. Bud never complained about an actual call. His verbal barrages were directed at all officials, all the time. So they never really bothered me because he had not learned that the only way to get to an official was to nag him about a blown call. Perhaps he did know, and just didn't want to pay us the final insult.

You can imagine how excited I was some 15 years later when, as the assistant director of officiating, I went to the Bomber office to meet their new head coach, Mike Riley, Bud's son. I could hardly wait; one Riley had been enough for me. Cal Murphy, the Bombers' general manager, was busy and pointed me in the direction of Mike's office. When I walked in, he immediately turned from the film he was watching, flashed a large smile and greeted me with the warmth and enthusiasm reserved for a long lost brother.

No one is this nice, let alone Bud Riley's son, I thought. I was sure I was being set up for later in the season when his true personality would come out. As luck would have it, the team started out doing well and his personality didn't change. But then it hadn't been tested. Finally, he had several losses in a row, one of which was not helped by a dubious officiating call, which may have changed the outcome of the game.

The timing couldn't have been worse. I was scheduled to appear on Cal Murphy's TV program along with Coach Riley the next night. Media criticism was growing, questioning whether Mike was too young to be a head coach. I sat directly across from him during the program. He looked more like a raccoon than a head coach; his eyes were blackened and his face was wearing the signs of a first-year head coach.

Thankfully, after the program, Mike was busy with the producer and I quickly headed for my car in the darkened CKND parking lot, avoiding what I'm sure would have been an ugly confrontation over our less than stellar officiating performance in his last game. As I reached my car, I heard the voice of Mike Riley in the darkness. "Neil, I'd like to speak to you." I quickly moved under the only light standard in the parking lot so my body would be easier to find when the ambulance arrived.

At last, the real Mike Riley. But there was no yelling, no screaming, no bitterness, no finger pointing, no swearing, only the same Mike Riley that I'd met several months earlier for the first time. Apologetically, he raised the issue of the blown call, not to complain about it, but to suggest how it could be avoided in the future. My earlier assessment of Mike Riley led me to conclude that coaches aren't the only paranoid people in the CFL.

In discussing the incredible differences between Bud and his son Mike, I suggested to Don Barker that as kids we observe our parents, and try to eliminate those characteristics in ourselves that we dislike in our parents. But I think Don correctly concluded that such a major transformation between Mike and his father could only be accomplished by his mother's incredibly strong genes.

Mike Riley completely destroyed the theory that good guys finish last. Not only did he win the Grey Cup, but he did it with a group of CFL loony tune characters, which included James "Wild" West, Tyrone Jones, Less Browne, and the rest of the ensemble, whose free spirits could not be controlled by any coach, let alone by themselves.

Every official, although few will readily admit, have a particular coach who, simply put, "gets to them." My nemesis was Jim Duncan, head coach of the Stampeders. Being a rookie was tough enough, but standing in front of Jim Duncan on the sideline was pure hell. After the first game, I was convinced that I was responsible for every problem that happened on the field. He started screaming and yelling from the opening whistle and only reluctantly took a break at half-time because he had to go to the dressing room. "Payne, they're offside. Payne you missed that pass interference. How could you miss that block? Get in the game…" And on and on. It never stopped.

Today when we interview officials for work in the CFL, I invariably ask whether they're bothered by coaches yelling at them. Inevitably they answer, "Not a bit." Either they're not being honest with themselves, or they have never worked in front of a coach like Jim Duncan.

I was convinced that as a rookie, Jim Duncan was testing me. But there was no way I was going to let the flag fly and let him know that he had me. And there was also no way I could continue to take the abuse. By the third game, things hadn't changed but quite frankly I couldn't understand a lot of the things he was complaining about. Sure, I knew when he complained about offside or procedure, but the missed blocks, broken plays and pass interference downfield were all a mystery. To make matters worse, he started screaming "Pine... Pine... Pine you missed that block." Hell, now he couldn't even get my name right. Little did I realize that he was yelling at one of his players, Rob Pine. The light went on. Coach Duncan was yelling at everyone, players and officials alike. It didn't matter who you were, it was your fault.

Finally, I penalized Duncan because he simply wouldn't shut up. But as Don Barker said, "It was like farting against thunder." It had absolutely no effect.

But justice was eventually served. A Calgary player had taken a penalty, and when the team came to the bench, Duncan wanted to know the perpetrator. No one came forward. Now incensed, he started shouting at referee Don Barker. "Barker...Barker...Barker come here I want to talk to you." Don was stationed comfortably at centre field, which in Canadian football is a long way from the sideline. He blissfully ignored coach Duncan's increasing pleas.

In complete exasperation, Duncan ordered his captain, Wayne Harris, who would never use one word if none would do, to go on the field and get the player's number from Barker, which he did and headed back to the bench.

It wasn't long before Jim was again on the sideline screaming even louder, if possible, for Barker to come to the sideline. Finally, Don made his way back to Duncan, who again demanded to know the number of the player who committed the foul. Don responded, "I told your captain."

Now all eyes were on Duncan, who sheepishly replied, "That's the problem; he won't tell me." Everyone had had enough, even the players.

Coach Hugh Campbell was at the other end of the spectrum. He was one of the most successful coaches in CFL history, and he used his considerable coaching skills to run the most envied franchise in the league, the Edmonton Eskimos. Hugh gave the appearance of being a simple, quiet man from the Midwest, with perhaps a little bit of cow manure still on his shoes. Nothing could be further from the truth. His fierce competitive nature is evident in the success he enjoyed as a player, and his six Grey Cup appearances as a coach.

My most memorable and perhaps most difficult encounter with Coach Campbell occurred in his first year as head coach, after his Eskimos were beaten in the 1977 Grey Cup by the Montreal Alouettes in the first "shoegate," where Montreal players allegedly puts staples in their shoes.

The officiating crew drove back to the hotel and with the pressures of the game and long season behind us, we were ready to let loose. By the time we hit the elevator in the hotel parking lot, we were, to say the least, a little more than boisterous. The elevator stopped at the main floor and when the doors opened our laughter hit the suffering Coach Campbell and his wife in the face. What a contrast in emotions. The elevator grew silent on a trip that seemed to last forever. After a complete study of the elevator ceiling, I found myself looking at Campbell. While his suffering was written all over his face, so was a determination that it wouldn't happen again. And it didn't. Edmonton won the next five Grey Cups under his leadership.

His competitive nature, although better disguised in his role of general manager, is probably matched only by that of Cal Murphy, the former general manager of the Bombers. For reasons probably known only to themselves, these two coaches have engaged in many battles, often reducing themselves to kids fighting over marbles, whether it was over what dressing room they would use at the Grey Cup, who would call the coin toss, or simply what colour uniforms they would wear, with cagey Hughey on one side and volatile Cal on the other, neither giving an inch.

As a coach, Hugh again tried to hide his competitive nature, presenting the officials with a simple, quiet, homegrown, folksy attitude, which again was miles from the truth. If you had a chance to check Campbell's home library, I'm certain you'd find its shelves stocked with psychology textbooks, some of which he could have written himself. For most coaches, officials were to be used for venting their frustration, or complaining about a blown call. To Campbell, complaining was an important part of the game, with the idea that officials, when properly massaged and brainwashed, might respond in a positive way to his psychological warfare at a critical point in the game.

Unlike most coaches who patrolled the sideline, you very seldom heard Hugh, but you knew he was there. When Edmonton was ahead by two or three TDs, which was often, you never saw him, but when the game was close, you knew Hugh would be around to help you with your officiating.

Suddenly you would feel his presence directly behind you. There was no yelling or bitching. Hugh would simply whisper in your ear. Instead of trying to shut out the yelling and screaming, I found myself straining to hear what he had to say.

Coach Campbell seldom complained about a blown call unless it was to set you up for something later in the game. The one yard between the offensive and the defensive lines and the motion in the Canadian game present numerous difficulties for sideline officials, but thankfully Hugh was always there to help out.

After a short yardage situation, which invariably would become an important factor later in the game, Hugh would whisper, "Neil, you know they were offside on that play. We both know they were offside; you've got to make that call." He was really hoping that later in the game, in a crucial situation, he would see a flag. It was a ploy used by many coaches, but none did it as well as Hugh.

He was also a master of reverse psychology, a quality reserved for the very best. "Neil," he would again whisper. "Can't you see their flanker is hitting the line too soon? Are you ever going to call it?" I would watch the flanker for the next several plays and while he was close, he certainly wasn't close enough to rate a penalty call.

But if you watched the Edmonton flanker, he was even worse, and maybe even illegal at times. Cagey old Hughey was saying if you don't call their flanker, then you can't call ours, even if what their flanker is doing was legal, and ours isn't.

In the Edmonton glory days, rival coaches and GMs would complain bitterly that Edmonton received special treatment from the officials, a theory that doesn't deserve comment. However I am convinced that like the excellence in other areas of the Edmonton organization, players and coaches knew how far to push the officiating envelope and stopped from going over the line where it would have drawn penalties. In fact, just as a team knows how its players will react in certain situations, Edmonton seemed to know how certain officials would react. They are, after all, only human and humans tend to act in a predictable manner.

Coaches who only occasionally complain about a player or the actions of another team are going to draw the official's attention, if only to ensure he is not missing something.

On the other hand, a coach who screams and yells and complains about everything, on every other play, is the big loser, because when he has a legitimate complaint it gets lost among all of the irrelevant bitching and complaining.

It is impossible to talk about Hugh Campbell without discussing Cal Murphy, probably the most controversial and colourful coach and GM in the league. The careers of Hugh Campbell and Cal Murphy are, in some respects, mirror images, both coaching together in Edmonton, both becoming head coaches and general managers of the teams they coached, both winning Grey Cups and both possessing a fierce, un-compromising, and unfailing competitiveness to win. It was this quality that would make them such bitter rivals. They were unable to agree on whether the sun was shining, let alone the more important things of life, like whether the offensive or defensive teams should be introduced at the Grey Cup.

In today's cautious and sterile world of being "politically correct," Cal was probably the league's most politically incorrect figure of the '80s and '90s, wearing and displaying his emotions on his sleeve. What you saw was what you got. There was no need to look at the scoreboard to know what end of the score his team was on. His face said it all, and when he was losing, both his players and the officials paid the price of his personal attention, which did justice to his Irish temper.

Cal spoke his mind, whether it was how the league should be run or whether female reporters should be allowed in the dressing room, which led his supporters to claim he was a man of principle, while others claimed he was a stubborn and cantankerous old man. Inevitably, it led to a love-hate relationship with the public, particularly in Winnipeg.

For myself, I'm not quite sure how I feel. I have gone through the full range of emotions with Cal, where one minute I'd like to hug him (well, not really) and another I'd want to wrap my hands around his neck but didn't because I knew they'd have a tough time getting my fingers unpried. Strangely, these emotions could and usually did occur over a period of fewer than five minutes, where one minute Cal would berate me about some past event with heated passion, followed by a compassionate understanding of some of our problems, with the original issue quickly forgotten.

One of the most difficult jobs as an officiating supervisor is to be confronted by a coach whose team has lost on what he believes to be a bad call. There was more than one such meeting with coach Cal, which were, to say the least, lively in nature, most times ending in disagreement as to what actually happened on the field. On occasion, these discussions came to an abrupt end when I admitted officials had erred and we were wrong, with further discussion concentrated on solving the problem.

I soon learned that whatever I discussed with Coach Cal went no further, even though he could have used it to deflect criticism away from himself if he had released it to the media. This integrity I'm proud to say exists almost universally among veteran CFL coaches and general managers, who have never publicly released the contents of confidential conversations to the media, even where it would have benefited their own careers.

Being a lifetime resident of Winnipeg, my association with Cal extends over some 20 years. Many of our meetings occurred on Sunday mornings when, as a supervisor, I attended church with some of the game officials before an afternoon game. Whether it was St. Ignatius or Holy Rosary in Winnipeg, or a Catholic Church in Calgary or Edmonton, Cal and his wife Joyce were invariably there.

We kneeled several rows apart, Cal praying for forgiveness for what he was going to say to the officials that afternoon, the officials praying that Cal wouldn't say anything, and me praying for a transfer to another CFL city, but knowing it wasn't going to happen, and finally resigning myself to "Lord, Thy will be done."

My first association with Cal came in the early '70s when I patrolled the sidelines and Cal was an assistant with Edmonton. My recollection of these early times is somewhat blurred, although my psychiatrist assures me that it is natural for the mind to block out unpleasant memories. As we both moved up the food chain, Cal as a coach, me as a referee, our contact became more direct. One of the benefits of being a referee is the opportunity to meet the head coach prior to the game at centre field, to discuss trick plays, get the numbers of team captains and of the quarterbacks and special teams.

The referee, as a courtesy, always speaks to the visiting team first. In Winnipeg, I used to face the Winnipeg end, while talking to the visiting coach at centre field. One look at Cal and you knew what happened the previous week. A win and he was relaxed, joking with his coaches; a loss and he was like a caged lion, waiting for his turn at the zebras.

Usually, the meeting with the visiting coach lasted longer than it should have. If it was Don Matthews, you could be sure it was because he was telling us another one of his corny jokes. By now Cal had changed from a caged lion to a raging bull, pacing back and forth pawing at the turf. I often wondered whether he would have charged if I had waved my flag.

After a loss there were no pleasantries, only a machine-gun attack on either the officials from the previous week, or on the tactics of the visiting team. Ross Perrier claimed he was successful in diffusing these situations by interrupting Cal and asking him how his wife and family were. This tactic didn't work in Hamilton, where after a Winnipeg loss Cal put his hands around Ross' neck and tried to squeeze the life out of him.

As a head coach in the '80s I don't think there was anyone more astute in the league. He seemed to know everything that was happening on the field, including every foul that wasn't called. Before every game he usually had some bizarre play he said he was going to try, from the centre snapping the ball and leaving it on his butt while everyone else ran around looking for it, or snapping the ball and putting it behind the guard's legs. The officials ended up running back to the dressing room where we held a lively discussion trying to determine whether Cal's new play was legal.

As a referee, I didn't benefit from the same intimate contact Coach Murphy shared with the sideline officials, but he knew how to get my attention. Late in the game, he would start looking for the call that might make a difference. When I got near the sideline, I knew I would benefit from his advice. "Fifty-four is holding. Make the darn call!" he would bark.

I knew No. 54 was doing some holding and Cal knew that I knew, and tried to work on me to make the call. It was the same holding we had permitted on both teams throughout the game, and to change the standard late in the game is a cardinal sin of officiating. The pressure was relentless, but once I heard, "Payne, you gutless wonder, make the call!" I knew it was his last hurrah because he had nothing further to add.

In Cal's defense, in all his sideline tirades I never heard him use any language you wouldn't use around the kitchen table, and when he really got mad the phrase "Jimminy Cricket" usually came into play. I couldn't believe his use of the Lord's name in a half-time television interview from Regina, and yes, I sent him the tape.

In 1984, one of my first duties as a supervisor was to visit the Bombers office and review game films. Incredibly, up until that time, officials had not reviewed any of their own performances, and had to take the media's word on how lousy we were. To Cal's credit he was one of the first coaches who insisted on providing officials tapes so we could review our performances.

Originally, we had no equipment, which meant doing the tape review in the teams' offices. I tried to sneak into the Bomber office unnoticed, without having to go nose-to-nose with Cal, but just like a dog who could smell the mailman coming, Cal was lying in wait. He appeared in the doorway with his own tape that he popped into the machine to show me a clip he thought the officials missed in the game when Winnipeg had played in B.C. When I suggested the block was from the side and, in fact, legal, I knew I was in trouble as I absorbed a barrage of criticism. I couldn't believe it; I thought I was back on the field, only this time I was cornered. I looked at the film and knew we were right and pushed back just as hard, even though I knew Cal and I would never agree.

I made up my mind that I wouldn't reduce myself to his level, but five minutes later I found myself screaming and yelling even louder than Cal. The meeting ended the same as all subsequent encounters, no matter how volatile, with Cal laughing and joking, and me with a headache. I can never remember leaving his office with any bitterness, even though some of the exchanges were loud and bitter. Often we were interrupted by either Urban Bowman or Mike Kelly, Cal's assistant, who came in during a lull in the action to see if we were both still breathing. This scenario was repeated on numerous occasions, with many things said in the heat of the battle, or in confidence, that were probably better not said. But never once was I concerned that our battles would go beyond his office, and they never did.

Being the supervisor of officials in Winnipeg when Cal was coach was a treat because he couldn't come up to the press box to get at us from field level. However, Cal as general manager was an entirely different matter. Even though he was no longer the coach, there was no doubt who was in charge, and he took great delight in aggravating the visiting teams, particularly the Eskimos and the Lions.

Early in the season, the B.C. Lions were visiting and, as usual, Cal was feuding with B.C. management over what I thought were recent player transactions. I was relaxing at half-time sipping on a Coke when a B.C. coach burst into our booth complaining that someone had turned off their dressing room lights. By the time I found an electrician and corrected the problem, it was too late; the teams were already back on the field. The B.C. coaching staff were livid because they were unable to make any half-time adjustments as they sat in the dark waiting for the lights to come on.

The electrician claimed one of the concession workers inadvertently turned off the switch to the B.C. dressing room, but I knew the concessions were nowhere near the light switch. My guess is that one of Murphy's relatives worked in the concessions.

When I told Don Barker the next day what had happened, he began to laugh, and related what had happened earlier when Winnipeg had visited B.C. for a game in July. It was an extremely hot day for Vancouver and as usual the stadium was considerably hotter than the 30 degrees Celsius outside. Cal, in his game of one-upmanship, rented two large fans to keep his players cool at the Bomber bench. Only there was a problem. Mike McCarthy, the B.C. general manager, wouldn't give Cal a place to plug them in. Cal finally found Don Barker, who was supervising the game, and in his typical Murphy manner started screaming and yelling that Mike wouldn't supply any power for his fans. As usual, when Cal started screaming and yelling, Don simply walked away. Finally Don caught up with Mike and said, "Mike, if you don't give Cal any power, you'll pay for it later." Mike gave him the power, but it looks like he paid anyway.

B.C. may have invented crowd noise and electronic devices to upset the visiting quarterback, but Murphy perfected it. The music in Winnipeg coincidentally appeared to start when the visiting quarterback got up over the ball. I knew Cal wasn't directly responsible, but he had orchestrated what was happening. Finally, after several games of detective work, I noticed Don Kirton, the field announcer, nod to Murphy, who was in his booth. Don then walked over to the Bomber bench and sure as hell, the music started seconds after he picked up the phone. I finally caught up with Don and asked him what was going on. He started to laugh and said, "Whenever I get a signal from Cal, I call the control booth and get them to play the music, which seems to happen just as the quarterback comes up over the ball."

Cal's temper was no less volatile as general manager. My modest supervisors' booth, which Cal had generously equipped with a 12-inch, reconditioned black-and-white TV to watch replays, was usually fully occupied with Winnipeg CFL officials who stood facing the field with their backs to the door.

We knew that on the first controversial play we'd receive a visit from Cal, who occupied a booth down the hall. Sure enough, the door would fly open and although we never saw him, we certainly heard him, as we braced for his verbal assault, which certainly would have shattered the windows in our booth had they not been open. No one would say word as he slammed the door and returned to his booth.

Not only did the guys know when he was coming, but they would bet on how long it would take him to get there. After a particularly bad call I jokingly yelled, "Lock the door," knowing the door had no lock. But Glen Johnson, a Winnipeg CFL official and a devil by nature, seized the opportunity to put his shoulder to the door and keep Cal out in the hall as he pounded on the door.

Cal was not alone in his visits to the supervisors' booths. Joe Kapp was just as zany as the general manager of the Lions as he had been as a player, and he tried to visit Don Barker in his B.C. Place booth after a controversial call. But unlike in Winnipeg, Don was able to lock his door. Undaunted, Joe went through the adjacent TV booth and started to crawl around the glass divider that hung over the field. Don knew if Joe got in to his booth, he would either end up on his back in the booth, or at field level 45 feet below. Like any quick-thinking official, Don pushed Joe back around the glass divider as he hung precariously over the field. If anyone was going to get killed it was not going to be Don.

Working under pressure usually reveals the worst or best in people and sometimes both. In the last game of the 1991 season, Edmonton was scheduled to play Winnipeg on the first Sunday afternoon in November. Weather at this time of year in Winnipeg is at best unpredictable, and the week before the game it was absolutely brutal. It had rained for three days, then turned into ice, which covered both end zones and parts of the sideline.

I made my way to the stadium on Saturday night, where an army of workers was using every conceivable device in an attempt remove the two inches of ice without damaging the artificial turf. But nothing worked. The wind was blowing from the north at 40 clicks, making the minus 5 degree temperature seem even colder. The lights from the 40-foot towers were barely visible through the driving snow. In short, it was a Winnipeg blizzard. Out of the shadows appeared Edmonton coach Ron Lancaster, shaking his head. "I've never seen anything like this. I don't see any way how we can play tomorrow."

I couldn't have agreed more, as we put our backs into the wind in an effort to keep from freezing as we watched the field crew hopelessly pick away at the ice, more closely resembling Robert Bird and his exploration party to the North Pole than a football grounds crew. I suggested we meet with Cal the next morning before the game to see if there were any way we could play the game.

The next morning Coach Lancaster and I cooled our heels waiting for Cal to return from church. We expected full cooperation from Cal because it was his problem. Instead Cal started our meeting by berating Ronnie for something he'd allegedly said to the media the previous week. I could see the whole thing going into the tank, but thankfully Lancaster's only concern was to play the game, if possible, and get out of town.

We all knew that the league and the Bombers could ill afford not to play the game, and there was no chance it could be played at a later date. My only concern was the safety of the players. I knew the end zones and sidelines were a sheet of ice and not safe. I spoke to the Edmonton players' representatives, expecting them to say that the field was unsafe and there was no way they would play, whereupon I was prepared to cancel the game. But it didn't happen. The players knew the financially strapped teams would be in trouble if we didn't play the game, and said they were prepared to go ahead if it were necessary, although the tones of their voices and the looks in their eyes expressed a real concern for their safety.

The ball was back in my court, with less than an hour to game time. Behind closed doors I finally got Coaches Murphy and Lancaster into the same room and told them we would play on a reduced field because the end zones and sidelines were unsafe.

It was easy to change the size of the field and eliminate the end zones by relocating them on the playing field, but many other areas were impacted, such as the point of kickoff, restricted penalties near the goaline, scoring on kick plays, and more importantly ensuring the game didn't turn into a farce. Within seconds the finest brains in Canadian football were at the blackboard, covering what appeared to be every possible situation that could occur as a result of the redesigned field, which was now being remarked as we worked out the rules. I have always considered myself an expert on rules, but clearly both Ron and Cal immediately recognized the impact and the limitations as we adjusted the rules for our new postage stamp field.

Within 15 minutes, we had agreed to the new set of rules, and were ready to try them on the field. Perhaps the biggest break of all was the absence of Hugh Campbell due to an urgent family matter. I knew full well he and Murphy would still be arguing over whether there was going to be a game. As we left the Bomber boardroom the media crowded around the door. I felt like a UN Ambassador, accomplishing the impossible.

I stood in the Bomber hall outlining the ground rules and how the game was to be played when Alan Watt, Edmonton's assistant general manager, pulled me aside. It was the first time since I met Alan that he wasn't smiling. He whispered in my ear, "Neil, Hugh Campbell just called and we're protesting the game." My stomach hit the floor. Both teams had just agreed to play the game by our new Hudson Bay rules and if I told Cal that Edmonton was protesting the game, he'd need another transplant, and the rest of us emergency medical attention.

I quickly turned to Alan and told him, "Forget it. Both teams have agreed to play," and we walked by Cal without saying a word. Thankfully, the game was played without any problems, and yes, Edmonton won. A Winnipeg victory, and I'd probably have been looking for new job because I threw Edmonton's protest in the garbage.

Of all the encounters I had with Cal over 25 years, the last one is the only one I'd like to forget. It was orchestrated by the famous "shoegate," when Edmonton destroyed the Bombers in the 1996 Western semifinal in Edmonton.

I was scheduled to supervise the game and early in the week Cal summoned me to his office to examine the footwear he intended to use. Make no mistake—Cal was no novice when it came to illegal footwear, with Jake Ireland catching Stan Mikawos wearing baseball shoes against Baltimore in the eastern semifinal the year before.

Cal again put the baseball shoes forward for approval, claiming his players had worn these shoes before, which came as no surprise. After again rejecting the baseball cleats, his inventory appeared to consist of just the standard shoes. He also expressed concern for what Edmonton would wear, which was not surprising considering their intense rivalry. When Cal called me in to approve his footwear, I should have known it was an omen of what would lie ahead.

In an attempt to avoid any possible problems and give Edmonton equal treatment, Dave Yule, the game referee, and I visited the Edmonton dressing room Saturday night before the game to examine their footwear.

We were overwhelmed by the arsenal of shoes they possessed; every type of shoe and cleat imaginable, some of which we had never seen before, and all requiring close inspection to determine if they were legal. They claimed they had acquired the shoes from all over North America, and it appeared they could outfit every team in the league. We returned to the hotel knowing that if they wore the shoes we had approved, there wouldn't be any problems. But would they wear them?

Early next morning, I was still lying in bed when the phone rang. I knew by the loud and persistent ring that it had to be Cal. Sure enough, he was still concerned about Edmonton's footwear and I agreed to meet him at the stadium.

We told Cal that Dave would examine the Edmonton player's shoes during the game if he received any complaints from the Winnipeg captains. But this didn't satisfy Cal.

Early that morning, Winnipeg reportedly had gone to a local Edmonton sporting goods store to purchase footwear, with a number of their executives carrying armfuls of shoes into the Winnipeg dressing room. After the inventory we saw in the Edmonton dressing room the night before, it looked like the Girl Guides getting ready to fight the U.S. Army, which was closely reflected in the game score.

In spite of Dave's numerous inspections of Edmonton footwear throughout the game, it would appear that perhaps Edmonton did use illegal footwear, as reflected by the claims of scratches on some of the Winnipeg players' arms, as well as comments attributed sometime later to an Edmonton player.

Winnipeg Assistant Coach Mike Kelly claimed the illegal footwear was in the equipment bag on the Edmonton bench and demanded I examine the bags. I was forced to ignore his pleas because the league had told me to stay out of the team bags, which I had no authority to examine or remove. If illegal footwear were used, then we didn't get the job done, and no matter what the excuses, I must take responsibility.

Unfortunately I have not seen Cal since "shoegate." I hope the matter has been put to bed, but I know better. The following year I sponsored a rule change that would banish a player from the game if he uses dangerous footwear, which may end future "shoegates," but don't bet on it.

Cal was stricken by a serious heart attack. After he recovered, he remained unchanged; still ornery, committed, understanding, stubborn, volatile, happy, with every emotion occurring within the space of one football game. When someone undergoes a major illness, staring death in the face, their lives often become cautious and measured. With Cal nothing has changed, and his new heart pumps to full capacity every day. His donor should rest assured that when Cal is called, the heart will have nothing left to give. In the final analysis, Cal was a victim of his own success. He probably stayed in Winnipeg too long, which in pro sports is eventually the kiss of death.

6

Life on the Sidelines

My first season was almost over, only one game to go, and while I was disappointed it was ending, I wasn't totally unhappy because I had taken just about enough advice from the benches, and besides, I had done a good job.

It seemed a perfect way to wind up the season, with a so-called nothing game (a term I would never again use in my 30 years with the league) between the two-and-eleven Bombers and the Eskimos, who were near the top of the league.

I was the only rookie on the crew. Bill Dell was the referee, along with Gib Seguin, who was also from the East. Both of them had stopped in Winnipeg to do the game while on their way to do the big game in Calgary the next day. Harold Ferguson and Ken Stein, probably the best downfield official in the league, filled out the crew. With the exception of me, the rookie, it was a group of solid veteran officials.

Unfortunately the crew didn't meet until several hours before the game, and we hadn't worked with each other before. It was a perfect recipe for disaster: an officiating crew that wasn't prepared, working a game where they had already decided nothing much was at stake. But I learned that night that for a professional football player, there is no such thing as a nothing game. Personal pride and their fierce competitive natures, the qualities that made them professionals in the first place, make them refuse to accept defeat.

The underdog Bombers pushed the Eskimos all over the field that night and victory was a certainty if they could overcome one final obstacle: the officials, which on that Saturday night proved to be an insurmountable task.

Everything that could go wrong did, and while it might be difficult to claim this as the worst officiated game ever, it would have had no trouble making the top two. Five minutes into the game, Lou Andrews, a Winnipeg receiver, tried to catch a pass with his chest because his hands were being held by Dick Dupuis, an Edmonton defender. There was no call and it was downhill from there. Several minutes later the Edmonton quarterback appeared to throw a pass from somewhere near the vicinity of the timer's bench, but incredibly no one saw him step out of bounds. Again, no call.

Winnipeg threatened to take the lead, but we quickly stepped in and when Paul Brule intercepted an Edmonton pass and flopped to the ground, got up and began to run unmolested to the Edmonton end zone. Someone blew a whistle. To this day, we still claim it came from the crowd. We brought the ball back and, of course, Winnipeg failed to score.

From that point every call, no matter how correct, went against the home team, and the hard-core 16,000 fans who hadn't deserted their team during the long disastrous season were becoming, to put it mildly, rather frustrated.

Just before halftime, the tiny stones started arriving from the heavens. I couldn't understand why it had taken so long, but soon realized that it took some time for the fans to come down from their seats and pick up the rocks that were on the running track, and return to their launching pads.

At halftime, we headed off to the dressing room to re-group. Our credibility was gone, but there was still time to work a strong second half and hopefully save the game. It didn't happen.

Early in the third quarter, another missed call and it was all over. Luckily I had not made any of the bad calls, and wondered how these veteran officials could screw up a game, especially in my hometown. I made up my mind to stay away from the rest of the crew and concentrate on the calls on my sideline, which was in direct conflict with officiating lesson number three. Officials, like players, are only successful when they work together as a team. Now it was every man for himself.

It didn't take long for disaster to strike. I moved off the line of scrimmage to cover a receiver downfield when the Edmonton quarterback appeared to cross the line of scrimmage to throw a pass. But I wasn't sure, and didn't react. My good friend Jake Scheirich was on the downs box and right on the line of scrimmage. After the play, I looked him in the eye and asked, "Was he over?" Jake didn't say anything; he didn't have to. He just looked to the heavens and rolled his eyes.

Shit, I blew one. And now I was no better than the rest of the crew. Little did I know that the film would show that the call was too close to make, and was one of a few times that we were actually right.

But the stage was now set for lesson number four. If you worry and think about the call you just made, then your next call will inevitably make everyone forget about the first one because it will be twice as bad. We didn't have long to wait.

Two plays later, I was still thinking about the Edmonton quarterback crossing the line of scrimmage, when Joe Fernandez, an Edmonton defensive back, plucked off a Winnipeg pass while he was lying on the ground, got up and ran 65 yards for a touchdown. What I didn't see was that he was contacted on the ground and the ball should have been blown dead. Where was the help when I needed it? Not only had I deserted the crew, they had now deserted me.

In two similar plays we brought back a Winnipeg touchdown they legally deserved, and gave Edmonton a touchdown that should have been blown dead. At this point, the crowd became uncontrollable and the sky became black with missiles that were being hurled from the stands, and I seriously doubted we'd make it back to the safety of the dressing room after the final whistle.

But wait, Winnipeg is pressing for a last-minute, winning touchdown, a chance to get out of here alive. Third down and Winnipeg has an open receiver in the end zone; all he has to do is squeeze the pigskin. But John Wydareny, an Edmonton defensive back who was beaten on the play, grabs the receiver and holds on for dear life. But we've come too far to turn back. There is no penalty call on the Edmonton defender.

Suddenly all the frustration of a losing season and incompetent officiating pushed the fans over the edge as they poured out of the stands in an attempt to get at the officiating crew. Luckily we made it almost unscathed back to the dressing room, but the stick crew wasn't as lucky.

Instead of dropping the yardsticks and making a run for it, they hesitated and were soon surrounded by a group of fans who wanted blood—anyone's blood.

I could never understand why the league dressed the stick crew in large gaudy capes in the likeness of the three Musketeers, but soon realized that they presented a difficult target in their wide capes, and in fact they resembled the Musketeers as they literally fought for their lives in an attempt to get to the dressing room, thrusting and paring with their newfound swords.

The usual post game chatter was replaced with a sickening silence, except for the odd feeble attempt to justify what we had done. But as professionals we knew we had failed miserably. It was something we would remember the rest of our lives.

Luckily for the rest of the crew, they were able to sneak out of town under the cloak of darkness. But as a Winnipeger, I would be forced to remain and take the media criticism and abuse that was both inevitable and well deserved.

Thankfully, there were no newspapers on Sunday and maybe by Monday, I thought, the criticism would have abated. Who was I kidding? I thought of buying all the newspapers that came off the press, but what was I going to do with a hundred thousand copies of the *Winnipeg Tribune* and *Free Press*?

I gingerly opened both papers to the sports section and there it was in bold print "Bombers Victims of Incompetence" in the *Tribune* and "Officials Escape With Their Lives" in the *Free Press*. Thirty years later I'd find out how accurate the *Free Press* headlines were.

Each newspaper devoted two full pages to the debacle outlining every officiating error or perceived error in great detail, together with biting and all too accurate criticism. Jack Matheson, the football writer for the *Tribune* went even further, boldly listing our names and our home cities, demanding that we all be fired.

Once again I had the same sick and empty feeling I had experienced some 48 hours earlier, only this time I felt naked and publicly exposed. Was Jack right? Should we be fired? Absolutely, if in fact this was the best officiating that were capable of producing. The rest of the crew were all respected veterans, who had all worked a Grey Cup with the exception of Harold Ferguson, who was about to get his opportunity. Ken Stein was a veteran of three previous Cups. Fortunately for these officials, they were able to officiate the following week and start putting the episode behind them.

But what about Payne? The rookie, would he survive? In the space of 24 hours my world was turned upside down; self-confidence was replaced by self-doubt. Did I just have a bad game, or did I lack the right stuff to work at the pro level? I would have to wait eight long months to answer that question, if in fact the league were prepared to give me another chance.

I hadn't spoken to Bill Dell for almost 20 years and I wondered how accurate his recollection was of that Saturday night almost 30 years ago. I called Bill and after the usual reminiscing, Bill somewhat guardedly, asked: "Neil, what do you want?"

Almost as reluctantly I said, "Bill I'd like to talk to you about a game we worked together." By then, I had proudly worked two Grey Cups with Bill, and the 1976 classic between the two Roughriders. But Bill knew exactly where I was going. "You mean the game in Winnipeg," he said.

Bill couldn't recall the other team, but like me he remembered all the ugly details. "That's the one where we had the phantom whistle," referring to the Winnipeg touchdown we'd called back. Together we were both transported back into the Winnipeg dressing room remembering all the details of events we had spent 30 years trying to forget. I now have some small understanding of the feeling and the pain of war veterans recalling the events that claimed their fallen comrades. I suddenly realized that rarely have I forgotten the officials that I have agonized with and suffered with when we had failed, but seldom do I remember the names of those I drank and laughed with after a solid performance. Even when hard pressed, I can't remember the names of the men I worked with in four Grey Cups, while the memory of that Saturday night, October 17, 1970, crew remains permanently part of my being.

I also made a mistake in calling Jake Scheirich to again discuss the details that we had buried that night, and found out more than I wanted to know. Jake recalled the stick crew trying to battle their way back to the dressing room when he was cornered by a group of fans. "They started to beat me over the head with a metal chair. I thought I was going to die. The crowd was insane. Out of nowhere Don Mazur (a junior football player who was as large as Chris Walby) jumped out of the stands, and saved my life." Typical Jake; when it happened he thought we had enough to worry about, so he remained silent.

Winnipeg winters, which are long and cold, were made even longer wondering about my future; worrying about whether or not I personally had the jam to work in the CFL, and whether I was going to be asked back.

Mercifully, Hap's invitation to return arrived in early January. Hap was a former official and Hall of Famer who realized if he fired every official who made a mistake, he would have to hire an entirely new staff every year. One problem solved; but was I good enough?

I'd like to tell you that in my first game back that I made three brilliant calls and lived happily ever after, but for all rookies that's simply not reality. It took five years before I could look in the mirror and recognize a competent and comfortable CFL official, stumbling a number of times along the way, but never forgetting the lessons of that October Saturday evening.

A sideline official in the CFL regularly makes up to 10 judgments on every play, which translates into 1,800 per game or about 35,000 a year. Inevitably there are questionable judgments, some that are minor, and others that will bury an official. But what about the good ones?

I'd like to tell you about all the great calls I made. There had to be some out of the 35,000 judgments I made every year, but quite frankly I've forgotten them; and who outside your officiating supervisor and your fellow officials really cares? The only time we pay attention to an official is when he makes an infrequent error, and then only to remind him of the shortcomings.

Every rookie official is guided by wily veterans who try to keep the "rooks" out of trouble—both on and off the field. Abe Kovnats, who was at that time a five-year veteran in the CFL, who I had worked with in amateur football in Winnipeg, and who has become now a good friend, decided he would be my guardian angel, a decision that on at least on one occasion almost got us both fired. Even though Abe was 10 years older, we were still both boys, who many suspected would never really grow up. The only difference was Abe knew every football coach, player, trainer and fan from Montreal to Vancouver, which was great if you're in politics but dangerous if you're a referee. Little did we know he was honing his skills and would soon become a colourful member of the Manitoba Legislature, as well as its deputy speaker.

When on the road, filling in time was always a challenge. Abe enjoyed long walks, and as a rookie it was my duty to follow my mentor. Our walks were punctuated by frequent stops, because Abe knew everyone, and he always had time to exchange life stories while I cooled my heels on the sidewalk.

One day in Regina, where we always had nothing but time on our hands, the boys once again took over. On one of our walks we stopped at Woolworth's and picked up a large bag of coconut marshmallows, for which we both had a weakness. As we walked down the main drag with bag in hand, the gauntlet was thrown. "I'll bet I can get more marshmallows in my mouth than you can," I said, and the battle was on.

The challenge was almost successfully completed when Norm Kimball, the GM of the visiting Eskimos, turned the corner and headed directly towards us. Norm had a genuine dislike for officials and normally wouldn't give us the time of day, but on this occasion he tried to exchange friendly greetings with Abe, having no idea who I was as I slid into the background.

Abe could only shake his head, and respond with the variety of facial expressions, finally pointing to his bulging cheeks as Mr. Kimball turned and walked away. You could tell by the expression on his face that we confirmed what he already knew; that officials were a few bricks short of a load. It also confirmed what I already knew; that Abe could get into trouble even when he kept his mouth shut.

But Abe's on-field help wasn't long in coming. He had done a good job as a downfield umpire, and had quickly become a referee. It was a Sunday afternoon game in Winnipeg with, yes, the visiting Eskimos, who by the fourth quarter had the game well in hand. They put the diminutive Larry Highbaugh, a defensive back, in on offense. It was like rubbing salt into the wound.

Larry lined up on my side, and sure enough, on the first play they threw to him. The Bombers also knew where the pass was going and had him surrounded. Somehow, the five foot six inch Highbaugh outjumped the entire Bomber defense, came down with the ball, and ran down the sideline for a touchdown.

But there was one small problem. I had gotten blocked out by the Bomber defenders and wasn't able to cover Highbaugh down the sideline. I thought he was out of bounds because he was close enough to shake hands with the fans in the first row as he crossed the goal line, but I was too far way to tell.

Mickey Doyle, the captain of the Bombers, who were now not only beaten, but embarrassed, complained bitterly to Abe that Highbaugh had stepped out of bounds. All Abe had to say was, sorry, we missed it. Or, yes the sideline guy blew it. Or the sideline official got blocked out of the play. But what does he say? In order to protect the rookie, he looked Mickey Doyle in the eye and said, "Serves you right for letting a little fart like that catch the pass," lecturing Mickey as only Abe could. Infuriated, Mickey could hardly wait to get back to the Winnipeg bench to pass on Abe's message.

I knew there would be a league investigation and even though I made the mistake, I knew Abe's ass was on the line for what he had said to the Winnipeg captain.

What do I do—lie and save both of us because only Mickey, Abe and I knew for sure what was said, or tell the truth and hurt the friend who was trying to save my skin? It was a no-win situation. The call wasn't long coming "Neil, this is Hap Shouldice. I'd like to ask you a question about the Winnipeg-Edmonton game." As I wondered what I would say, he continued, "Did you hear Johnny Stroppa tell the Bombers that they blew the play for letting Highbaugh catch that pass?"

Johnny Stroppa? I thought. He wasn't anywhere near the play. "No," I said, in complete honesty.

He thanked me and promptly hung up, and I never heard another word. I can only conclude that Hap would never put an official in a position to bury a fellow official for what was said in the heat of the battle.

The episode didn't slow Abe down. When the league equipped referees with microphones it provided Abe with another platform to further develop and extend his already extensive communication skills. Initially the referee had no control switch and the microphone provided a direct line into the CBC television booth. Abe regularly entertained the television crew with his humorous and verbal jousting with players and coaches, until the microphone was equipped with an on/off switch, over the protestations of the CBC, who could no longer eavesdrop on the entertaining and heated arguments, the contents of which should never have left the field of play.

Don Wittman, a veteran CBC sportscaster, recalled one evening in Winnipeg when Charlie Libel, a rookie official, made what appeared to be a less than accurate call. Again Mickey Doyle, the Winnipeg captain, was incensed and was standing next to Abe, who was refereeing. Doyle called Charlie an asshole. Witt was listening to Abe through the referee's microphone and recalled Abe turning to Mickey and saying, "You may think he's an asshole, and I may think he's an asshole, but you can't call him an asshole." Whereupon Abe picked up the ball and marched off a ten yard penalty against the Bombers, while Witt fell apart in the booth.

When I became a referee, an on/off switch didn't solve my problems because every once in a while I would leave the switch on after I announced a penalty. Not only was the microphone live for the fans in the stands but also over the live television for the folks at home.

I can recall one game in Montreal where Edmonton was the visitor and the game was marred by controversy because the Montreal ground crew kept opening the doors at the end of Olympic Stadium to create a wind tunnel in the end zone when Edmonton came close to the goal line. After three and half hours of bitching and complaining, Montreal had the game well in hand. With less than two minutes to go everyone was ready to go home including the teams.

Edmonton punted the ball to Montreal, who would have been content to run out the clock. Instead, Larry Rohan threw his flag for a meaningless illegal block. It was the last thing we needed. The players were becoming frustrated and hostilities and were threatening to break out all over the field. Larry had to come from downfield to report the call. When he got within hearing range, I yelled at him, "I don't care what you got, stick that flag up your ass!" I was getting as frustrated as the players.

What I didn't know was that my microphone was still on and my directions respecting his flag were broadcast nationwide. After the game, the crew tried to unwind at a bar in the Bonaventure Hotel, but we were soon told that we had consumed all their beer and we had to find a new watering hole. The next day, Ross Perrier called and said that after I made my infamous comment, the TV announcers had said that all the crew was interested in was getting the game finished so they could have a beer. Little did they know how right they were.

Every organization has one person whose sole purpose is to drive management crazy. Abe was self-delegated to carry out that task on behalf of the officiating staff, a role he fulfilled with flair and imagination. Abe knew every equipment manager in the league and by the time he completed his first tour of duty he was in possession of a monogrammed sweatshirt from every team in the league.

Out of respect for the competing teams, Abe would wear one of the sweatshirts under his officiating jersey, usually the home team's. Finally, on one of his infrequent visits out west, Hap came down to our dressing room before the game, and there was Abe, decked out in one of the competing teams sweatshirts. Understandably, Hap almost had a coronary, and after a quick meeting between the two, Abe removed the shirt, but later continued to wear it, only inside out.

Abe's penchant for trying to help people and his fetish for footballs proved to be a lethal combination. The Winnipeg football club had expressed concern that game balls seemed to be disappearing from the officials' dressing room after the game.

Abe was involved in his community's amateur football program, and like most amateur groups, funds had run out. No more money for balls. No problem, Abe would look after it. Before the season was over half the amateur teams in Winnipeg were using CFL balls.

Officials were also his benefactors. After the crew's last game in Winnipeg on the night before Halloween, the crew returned to Abe's home to celebrate, and when Abe loaded the crew on the airplane early the next morning he gave them all gigantic pumpkins which they carried on their laps contrary to airline regulations, because they were too big for the overhead. It was a good thing the season ended before Christmas because the crew would've ended up dragging Christmas trees on board from Abe's tree farm, which he generously provided to anyone in need.

But it was Abe's fetish for footballs that finally caught up to him, costing him a Grey Cup assignment. Make no mistake, Abe was a good official, having had a great season working as a field judge, and we all thought he would get and deserved the Cup assignment.

It was a late season game, again in Winnipeg, when during a time out a fan jumped out of the stands and onto the field. He was a big sucker, and everyone left him alone until he grabbed the ball and headed for the end zone. Players and officials stood and watched as he got near the goal line, but not Abe. He took off after the perpetrator, showing speed I might have imagined he possessed in his playing days. Relying on his football experience he tackled the fan from behind, dropping him like a large redwood. Abe quickly got to his feet and placed his knee across the now surprised and incapacitated would-be thief's windpipe.

As Abe patiently waited for the arrival of the Winnipeg security, knee still firmly placed, the intruders facial hue passed through three distinct colours of the rainbow. Finally, security dragged the almost totally limp fan off the field, with Abe now in possession of the football. Unfortunately for Abe, the game was nationally televised, and the league brass watching in Toronto were not impressed. Any chance Abe had of doing the Cup was gone. I often wondered what happened to that ball.

Officials, for whatever reason, can be their own worst enemy, particularly when faced with something new that coaches and players had spent weeks scheming over in the hope of beating the rules and gaining that little edge that might mean the difference between victory and defeat.

In a late 1974 season game in British Columbia with the visiting Eskimos, both teams battled and clawed in a well-played contest, with B.C. finally starting to take charge. Tom Cheney, a lifetime sideline official, had been asked to referee because of the retirement of some senior officials.

I was on the sideline and things couldn't have been better. The game was close and the teams were sticking to their knitting. Edmonton was third-and-two on their own 40 when they decided to gamble. They were only down a couple of points and, as far as I was concerned, it was far too early to start gambling. As usual, the yard between the offensive and the defensive lines shrunk, as I peered down the line of scrimmage ready to mark forward progress to see if Edmonton would make the first down.

I could hear Tom Wilkinson, the Edmonton quarterback, barking out the signals when the entire B.C. defensive line went offside, with the Edmonton centre still over the ball. I waved timeout with my flag and reported to Cheney, "The entire B.C. line is offside." He promptly moved the ball up five yards and signaled first down for Edmonton, while the B.C. players mumbled something about being drawn offside by the Edmonton quarterback.

I thought I would try and keep an eye on Wilkie to see what was happening. Sure enough, later in the same drive on a second and eight, Wilkie, while using his usual cadence, gave a quick "Hut, hut" while bobbing his head and shoulders as if to take the snap which never came. But the B.C. defensive line sure did. I threw my flag and hurried to tell Cheney what had happened.

By now the B.C. players were incensed about being drawn offside for the second time with a tactic neither the players nor officials had ever seen before. Wilkie's actions were not specifically covered in the rulebook, but I tried to tell Tom that the Edmonton quarterback was drawing B.C. offside, while the B.C. players were screaming in both of our ears.

A decision had to be made: take control and penalize Wilkie for drawing B.C. offside, putting an end to his herkey jerky action, which was clearly an unfair tactic; or continue to penalize B.C.

We chose the latter. What a mistake. For the rest of the game, Wilkinson had the B.C. defensive line on a string, twitching and jerking with every sound or movement he made, as if they had acquired a new mysterious neurological disorder, and frequently going offside.

By the fourth quarter the game was in shambles and I stopped calling offsides unless the B.C. player was in the Edmonton back field when the ball was snapped.

I was convinced the league would take immediate action to put an end to Wilkinson's newfound tool. But no. While Rome fiddled, Wilkie took his prototype movements and finely tuned them to a masterful art that was difficult to detect, but had the same devastating results.

The rules were finally modified but Wilkie persisted, seldom being called. In 1977, when I became a referee, I was going to do what I was not allowed to do on the sideline: stop Wilkie from drawing the defense offside.

Initially, I concentrated on every move Tom made over the centre, to the point where my eyes were fully open in a fixed position. Finally I made the call. You'd think I had insulted his mother. Within seconds he was all over me. "I've been doing this for the whole game and you didn't make the call. What the hell is the matter with you guys, you're so damn inconsistent you're nothing but a bunch of..."

He was right. He was so damn good that he rarely stepped over the line, making us look inconsistent when we finally did catch him. I called Wilkinson when I could, which was very infrequently, and often wondered whether it was worth all the abuse.

Some 15 years later the problem still hadn't disappeared. In the early '90s it became an epidemic. When reviewing a film I noticed Danny McManus, the veteran Edmonton quarterback, had the defense jumping offside with his movements. With today's scientific approach to the game and the teams incessant review of game films, it didn't take long for them to discover that we weren't making the call for drawing the defense offside. Soon the entire ensemble, including Slack, Garcia and Flutie, were developing their own style, each with varying degrees of success.

Doug Flutie had taken the art a step further and developed at technique to draw the defense offside from the shotgun position. As he called signals from about six yards behind the centre, he would simultaneously move his right foot forward and thrust his hands forward to catch the ball from the centre. The defense came, the ball didn't, resulting in a defensive offside.

I was there 25 years earlier when Tom Wilkinson drew the defense off for the first time and, later as a referee, I was still unable to stop Wilkie and his antics. Now as part of the supervisory staff, I had one last chance. At the end of the 1995 season we told the coaches we were going to penalize quarterbacks for any illegal movement, with zero tolerance. Recognizing the problem, the coaches agreed, and finally, after two years, it appeared we might just be winning.

Every time I see a lineman drawn offside I can't help but think we could of saved ourselves 25 years of aggravation if, on that sunny Sunday in B.C., we had penalized Tom Wilkinson instead of the Lions.

7

Pressure

Players and officials experience the same game-associated emotions. Several days before the game, your thoughts start shifting toward it, no matter what you're doing. This is definitely not a good time to be using your electric saw. The morning before the game, my stomach reminds me that it's getting close to show time. Even after 25 years, pre-game nervousness was a constant reminder of what was coming, and without it, an official should be looking for another line of work.

Our pre-game meeting was usually about six hours prior to the game. There, we discussed the teams, our coverage, the weather, trick plays and any other information that might impact the game. It also marked the beginning of the countdown to opening kick-off, where every officials focus was on preparing for the opening kick-off. For me, that also coincided with the tightening of the knots in my stomach.

Our meeting was followed by our pre-game meal at a moderately priced local restaurant, exposing the differences in men and their emotions. For some of us, it resembled the last supper. Normally, eating for me is a delight, with no amount or type of food going unchallenged. But before a game, food was simply a necessity if I was going to get through the next six hours. On more than one occasion, chewing my soup was even difficult and crackers were out of the question.

For others, the meal more closely resembled a medieval feast. Bill MacDonald, a veteran sideline official, could inhale his generously portioned meal before Ken Lazaruk could arrange his food in neat rows, no doubt in anticipation of helping the rest of us who couldn't finish our meal.

While we attempted to do everything as a crew we usually left Laz back in the restaurant still working delicately but diligently on his main course. Our early departure from the restaurant was the only way we could keep Bill from eating himself out of his uniform. I guess it was inevitable when Bill retired that he would become the M & M meat tycoon in Edmonton.

The mood at the restaurant was equally as varied. Most of the guys would engage in the usual small talk about their families and why the Maple Leafs were still in last place, all in an effort to relax. For me it was too late, the game controlled my every thought, and even if someone had told me that I won a million dollars, I wouldn't have heard them.

Two hours prior to the game we made our way to the stadium to begin what seemed an interminable wait. Even after checking out the field and blowing up the balls, we still had an hour until game time. Everyone went through their own ritual of getting dressed, some waiting until the last moment, while Ross Saunders rubbed homemade potions all over his body to protect not only its physical well-being but to drive away the bad calls. In reality these potions were only effective against Winnipeg mosquitoes, which was actually a welcome bonus. Fully dressed, we all sat in our favourite spots, waiting for the five-minute warning. If you weren't ready to do the game when you walked into that dressing room it was too late.

Years later, as a supervisor, we would frequently see the work of good officials quickly deteriorate for no apparent reason. When Don Barker or I contacted the official, the problem was inevitably linked to recent family or personal problems, or was job-related, where the official no longer had his family's support, or other problems preoccupied his thoughts.

Officiating is a brutal and demanding business, and unless you're able to devote your total concentration you simply can't succeed, and all too often even that's not good enough.

Close to game time, the constant buzzing is replaced with almost total silence, except for a couple of members of the crew who continue their meaningless chit-chat, while the rest of us sit in silence, either looking at the floor or nervously throwing a game ball from one hand to the other. I had my favourite corner in every stadium where I nervously yawned, waiting for the buzzer. Twenty years later, scientists discovered that yawning was beneficial as it provided more oxygen to the brain. Thank God, because I needed every advantage I could get.

The game buzzer in the dressing room ignited the adrenaline in your body. As we made our way through the tunnel I always had a strange mix of emotions: large doses of confidence, still encumbered with nervousness, and yes, even a bit of fear that I will fall on my face.

When you hit the field there's another boost of adrenaline, and any negative thoughts are now replaced with the excitement and challenge to control the adrenaline and work your ass off for the next three hours. As the crew stood on the sidelines waiting for the anthem, you'd catch the eye of a player which reflected your own emotions; a total commitment to do the best job you can for the next three hours, leaving nothing on the field when the game is over.

Once the game starts the players have the advantage. They can immediately relieve the tension and nervousness on the first play, with a block, tackle, or simply yelling at their opponents. For officials it isn't quite that simple. Just like the players, we want to get into the game by ruling on a tight sideline pass, a fumble, or anything where you have to take charge, and yes, even a penalty flag. All too often as a sideline official I would watch the play take place on the other side of the field, which in the Canadian game could be in another municipality, just waiting for something to happen. Play after play I'd raise my arms to shoulder height resembling a scarecrow in a farmers field, wondering when a flock of birds would arrive, and hoping they wouldn't poop all over me.

The longer you waited to "get in the game" was directly proportional to the degree of difficulty or the bizarre play that you would eventually be required to handle. I can remember Calgary playing in Winnipeg when, for almost the entire first quarter, every play, partly because of the wind, was on the other side of the field. I didn't even have an offside or procedure call, which in Canadian football is unthinkable. As the quarter came to a close, the pressure began to build as I repeatedly tried to warn myself to be ready, to stay in the game.

Finally it happened; a routine Bombers sweep to my side with the ball carrier coming directly at me. He was soon tackled. I ran in to blow my whistle. Just as I began to blow, and I mean the air had entered the chamber, out of the corner of my eye I caught the Bomber offensive lineman running past me with another ball. I sucked all the air out of the whistle and watched the Bomber lineman lumber 50 yards undetected by the Calgary defence.

I was so anxious to get in the game that I almost committed the cardinal sin of football officiating: blowing my whistle without seeing the ball. The man who I thought had the ball lay ball-less on the ground (gender slur not intended).

How did the offensive lineman get the ball? A new play had been invented where the centre snapped the ball and a quarterback convinced everyone including the officials that he handed off to the running back. Instead, the centre never gave the ball to the quarterback but instead lay it down behind his left leg. A few seconds later, the lineman picked it up and proceeded unmolested downfield. If I'd blown that whistle, I might as well have given it to the Winnipeg police chief for the traffic cop on Portage and Main, because I wouldn't have had another chance to blow it.

The last three minutes of a tight game, particularly a playoff game, provide the ultimate challenge for an official. At that moment, all his strengths and weaknesses are exposed for everyone to see. The adrenaline is now being pumped through your body with every heartbeat. Not only do you have to make the right call, but you are faced with the knowledge that any call may determine the outcome of the game, and it better be right. At this point for some, managing their own emotions becomes more of a challenge than making the call.

As a referee, you come face-to-face with every official who makes a critical call in these pressure-packed situations, sometimes learning more about their character, and even their soul, than you wanted to know. Good officials thrive in this type of environment, taking charge when necessary, and willing to put their careers on the line with their judgment, while others play it safe, making critical judgments only when forced.

I used to enjoy working with Larry Rohan when I refereed because on every play, particularly those that were critical, Larry could be counted on to step forward, take charge and tell you what happened, even if you didn't want the help. I was envious; the more important the play, the more relaxed he became, and perhaps not surprisingly more accurate, while most of us battled to stay under control.

Late in the season, B.C. had to beat Edmonton to get into the playoffs, and they were down near the goal line driving for the winning score. Larry was working downfield, and we had a rookie on the sideline. As the ball carrier passed the rookie, he followed him down the sideline, and as he was being tackled, the ball squirted loose on the ground, with both teams in hot pursuit. Larry, who was a good 20 yards away, sprinted to the spot where the ball was fumbled (sprint is probably too generous a term because Larry rarely got out of low gear) but nonetheless he got to the spot and ruled the ball dead before the fumble, claiming the ball carrier's knee was on the ground a split second before the ball came loose.

Edmonton had recovered the ball but Larry was no longer visible as he was mobbed by Edmonton players screaming for his scalp, while he calmly continued to mark the spot where he'd ruled the ball dead. Why had he run 20 yards to make the call on a play covered by another official? It wasn't his responsibility, so why do it, particularly if he knew that if he were wrong it would probably cost him his job? Because he knew he was right, and that's what good officials do.

I asked the rookie, "What happened?" I didn't have to wait for an answer. The look on his face told me that he didn't know whether the ball was fumbled before or after the ball carrier's knee hit the ground, and he had probably frozen on the play. We went with Larry's whistle, which thankfully for everyone turned out to be correct, and I learned that I had a veteran who was prepared to lay it on the line, and a rookie who didn't look like he would make the grade. Eventually though, the rookie learned from his mistake and is still working in the league today. Not only did Larry save the game, but probably the rookie's career as well.

Others were not so fortunate. The ability to handle the stress and pressure will often determine whether an official can make it at the professional level. The professional careers of many outstanding amateur officials are cut short because they're unable to adapt to the numerous pressures of the pro game.

CFL officiating clinics will often feature sports psychologists such as Cal Botterill, who also helps NHL players and Canadian national team members manage and control all the outside pressures. For most, the breathing exercises, mind control, physical conditioning, and positive thought processing provide some measure of success. For others, no amount of training, hard work and dedication will equip them with the tools needed to handle the job of a professional official.

It's easy to recognize people in our day-to-day lives who can't handle the pressures of stressful situations. Psychologists tell us that these people, more often than not, when put under pressure, are forced by their very nature to act immediately, to do something, anything, usually without analyzing the situation, which for an official can be disastrous, particularly when your only course of action is to throw a flag or blow a whistle.

Late in a game in Shreveport, LA, I was refereeing a game that, thankfully, was not being televised, when the Shreveport quarterback threw a sideline pass. Both the receiver and defender jumped up for the ball, drawing an immediate flag from the back official. In attempting to catch the pass, both the defender and the receiver bumped each other. Feeling the pressure of the situation, the official knew something happened, and reacted the only way he knew how, by throwing his flag.

As he approached me to report the call, I knew we were in trouble. I had seen that blank look before. "What do you have?" I asked.

There was no response. I repeated the question. Still no answer. He had seen something, the pressure made him react, and now he was trying to figure out what he had really seen.

I tried to help, telling him if he wasn't sure that I'd waive off the flag. But for him to admit he was wrong was to admit he couldn't handle the pressure of the pro game, and he quickly told me he had pass interference, still not knowing what happened, or even the number of the players involved. Unfortunately, the situation repeated itself later in the season with the same disastrous results; flags being thrown when there were no fouls on the play.

It had become obvious that even though he was an outstanding amateur official and had worked hard for several years in the CFL, he could not handle the pressure. Now came the always difficult task of releasing the official, all of whom are proud men. But when the axe fell, the official was relieved, because we had found out what he already knew: he couldn't handle pressure of pro football.

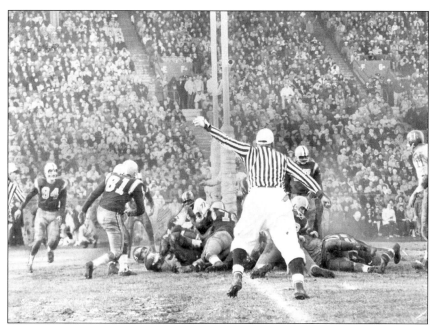

Paul Dojack signalling the winning Winnipeg touchdown in the 1959 Grey Cup.
(Courtesy *Winnipeg Free Press*)

It's not a stick-up but Rollie Miles of the Edmonton Eskimos scoring a TD against
Winnipeg in the 1953 final. (Courtesy *Winnipeg Free Press*)

Prime Minister Lester B. Pearson kicks–off while referee Al Dryburgh looks on at the 1966 Grey Cup. (Courtesy *Winnipeg Free Press*)

Neil Payne (far right) is helped off the field after being injured in the 1976 Grey Cup as Floyd Cooper No. 41 gets ready to take his place and Bill Dell looks on.

The referee gets to meet all the celebrities. Dick Assman of Dave Letterman fame tosses the coin for Saskatchewan's Ray Elgaard as Payne looks on. (Courtesy *Regina Leader-Post*)

A rumble in Birmingham with Payne getting buried at the bottom of the pile as Rick McFadyen No. 26 and Gary Cavaletto try to maintain order.

Payne waiting for repairs as Tony Michalek No. 28 and Cavaletto (bottom left) try to keep things under control while McFadyen wonders if he'll get a chance to referee.

Repairs completed and the crew ready to go.

Role reversal as official Jacques Decarie is bear-hugged by Montreal Concordes Harold Woods in a 1983 game against Ottawa. (Courtesy CFL)

1976 Grey Cup crew: No. 41-Floyd Cooper, No. 20-Jacques Decarie, No. 37-Neil Payne, No. 39-John Stroppa, No. 25-Bill Dell, No. 26-Don Barker, Hap Shouldice (Director of Officiating), Harry Ross (E.F.C. Supervisor) Don King (W.F.C. Supervisor).

Payne trying to keep track of Doug Flutie in the 1994 Labour Day Classic.
(Courtesy CFL)

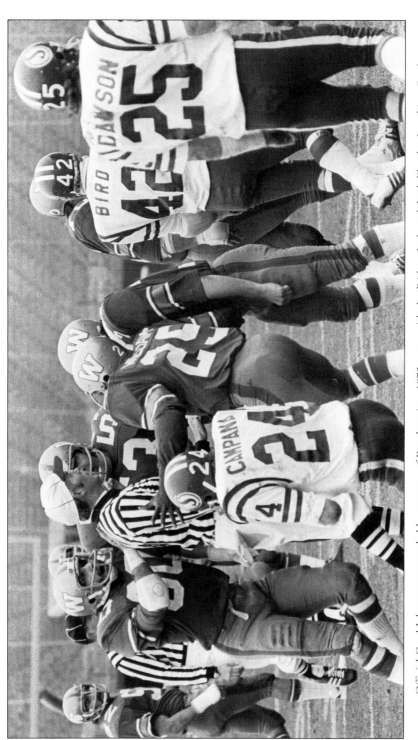

Official Gord Johnson surrounded by a group of Bombers in a 1973 game with the Riders. It doesn't look like they're asking Gord out for a drink after the game.

Zoo keeping is only part of an official's duties as Frank Chapman tries to get the Tiger Cat's mascot off the field. (Courtesy CFL and John Sokolowski)

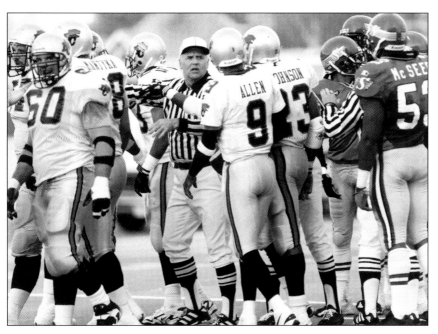

Umpire Ken Picot in the middle of the B.C. Lions can't believe what he just heard.
(Courtesy CFL and John Sokolowski)

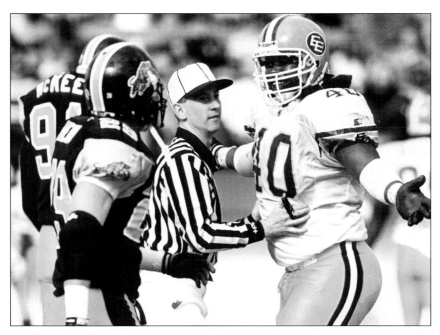

Field Judge Kim Murphy tries to help Edmonton's Bennie Goods out of trouble.
(Courtesy *Hamilton Spectator*)

Referee Jake Ireland covering Winnipeg's Kerwin Bell in a 1999 game against Hamilton. (Courtesy CFL and John Sokolowski)

8

Where's the Beer?

Once the final whistle blows, the pressure and stress are immediately exorcised from your body, but the adrenaline remains. The type of job the crew did on the field is immediately reflected in their mood in the dressing room. There is no greater feeling knowing that you have done a good job, and stayed out of the way of the teams. After the post-game shower, the crew, with supervisor in tow, returned to the hotel to dissect the crew's performance in an exercise closely resembling a public Catholic confession.

Every game without exception has several close or controversial plays, and officials would describe what they saw or didn't see in order to help the supervisor evaluate the game film the next day.

The difficult part came when the official was asked to reveal any problems they had that we hadn't discussed or that no one else had spotted. Replies and attitudes were extremely varied. Those of us who were taught by the Jesuits confessed freely, hoping to escape further recrimination. Others, trying to protect their own skins, provided only name, rank, and serial number, challenging the supervisors to find their mistakes on film. I'm not sure what was the best method, but invariably if you screwed up and the supervisors didn't catch it, one of the teams would, and then the shit really hit the fan.

Once the supervisor left and closed the door behind him, the mood in the room was immediately transformed into a post-war celebration by a group of men who jointly shared the pain and ecstasy of being professional football officials. Early in my career, after several post game bonding sessions, I attempted to avoid the inevitable damage to my brain cells and went to bed immediately after the game. My body twitched and turned like a tight spring trying unsuccessfully to unwind after the game, while my mind bounced off the ceiling and four walls like an energized ping pong ball, replaying every play, every call I made, and those I didn't. Sleep was impossible.

I soon learned that our post-game rituals were not only beneficial, but just like those damn salmon swimming upstream, unavoidable—in spite of the self-inflicted damage to our bodies. The most important off-field function for any rookie is the icing of the beer for the post-game ritual. It's a skill that has been passed down from official to official, which insures that once the beer is iced, just prior to leaving for the game, it will remain so until the sun comes up the next morning.

The ritual commences when, with beer in hand, the crew openly discusses its performance and challenges each other when they don't deliver. A four-beer meeting was not unusual after a particularly bad game. Officials who didn't get the job done were given a kick in the pants, hard enough to wake them up, but also carefully placed to ensure no permanent damage.

Rookies were the major benefactors from these meetings. In between keeping the veterans supplied with cold beer from the hotel room bathtub, there was enough time for the veterans to help them with the things they had done wrong three hours earlier, and give them the confidence and direction they so desperately needed.

Sometime after midnight, someone would realize that it had been over 12 hours since we had eaten, sparking a pilgrimage to our favourite local restaurant, which was usually the only one that was still open.

In Vancouver, we shared our steak soup and ranchero burgers at the Black Angus with the people who came out only after midnight. In Regina it was the Copper Kettle with Bob, the owner, who supplied his 20-pound pizzas, which eliminated any further digestion for 24 hours.

When we returned to the hotel a major decision was required. Everyone usually had an early morning flight, leaving three or four hours to solve the officiating problems of the league or to go to bed for several hours, desperately trying to fall sleep. A quick check of the bathtub supply influenced our decision.

Whether you went to bed or stayed up, the effect on your body wasn't much different. When you arrived home the next morning, with your wife mercifully waiting for you at the airport, all the adrenaline and energy had been drained from your body. After a quick coffee it was off to the regular job, for the longest and most painful day of the week, which on occasion I thought would never end.

Dragging myself home, I faithfully vowed every week that I would never again punish myself with these crazy post-game rituals, knowing full well that just like the salmon I had no other choice. After some 200 games and 20 years, I know I wouldn't have wanted it any other way.

Not surprisingly, over the years our high jinks took some unanticipated turns and ended in some rather bizarre places. Mid-week games in Edmonton were not my favourite assignment, because the flight back to Winnipeg left the next morning shortly before 7 a.m. The problem of the early flight time was further compounded by the almost hour-long bus ride to the Edmonton airport. Even if you got to bed early and you were fortunate to get a couple of hours of sleep, you had to drag yourself down to the lobby by 5 a.m. to catch the bus to the airport.

I was scheduled to work a Wednesday game in Edmonton when a last-minute crisis at work meant that I absolutely had to be there the following morning, unless I desired to change my line of work. I didn't want to bail out on the crew at the last-minute, and decided to take my chances with the early morning flight.

As much as I needed my sleep after the game, I wasn't prepared to take a chance on a couple of hours of shut-eye and miss my bus to the airport. By 3 a.m. the rest of the crew deserted me and went to bed. I sat on the edge of my bed desperately trying to stay awake until it was time to go down to the lobby.

Still not wanting to take any chances, I went down to the lobby early, and when the elevator doors opened I was faced with a lobby full of bags and people who were already getting on the bus. I quickly checked out and threw my bags in the baggage compartment and climbed aboard, happy to get a seat. I had taken the bus many times but this was the first time there were more than one or two people heading for the airport at this ungodly hour.

After performing the usual number of gyrations and manoeuvers required to escape the Château La Combe, we were on our way. Time to catch some sleep and the moving bus soon did its job. Sometime later I awoke and noticed we were on the highway getting close to the airport. Strange; I didn't recognize any of the usual landmarks, which had become familiar after numerous trips. I suddenly realized that I didn't recognize the highway either.

I was only two or three rows behind the driver and apprehensively shouted in his direction. "How long before we get to the airport?" almost fearing his response.

"Airport?" he said. "We're on our way to Yellowknife."

"Stop the bus!" I yelled as I jumped to my feet, stumbling into the aisle because my foot had fallen asleep.

Thankfully, the bus driver didn't follow my pleadings and instead pulled into an all-night service station. While the driver pulled my bags from the belly of the bus, I called a cab which I swear must have been following the bus, because it seemed to appear in a matter seconds, equipped with a hyper driver.

After wishing my fellow passengers a short farewell, with bags in hand, it was double-time to the airport, pleading with my driver to put the pedal through the floor. He managed to keep four wheels on the road, repeatedly trying to suggest in his own unique accent "Oh no man, can't go too fast," as even the billboards became a blur in the early morning light.

I have no idea where he picked me up, but if you catch a cab at the Edmonton airport, head for Yellowknife and stop when the meter reaches seventy dollars, then you've reached the spot. With only forty dollars in my pocket I quickly made arrangements to send him the balance and frantically ran to the gate, certain my plane had already left. Luckily the flight had been delayed and I arrived just in time. My job was safe for another week.

Who would believe that two buses from the same company were scheduled to leave 15 minutes apart from the Château at five in the morning? Twenty-five years later I still haven't been to Yellowknife and can't help wondering if I missed the opportunity of a lifetime.

There are times, though, when being a referee can be a help—even off the field, as the officiating crew at the 1983 preseason All-Star game in Vancouver in 1983. The game and festivities were a fun event for both players and officials. The game was set for Saturday afternoon and the crew arrived late Friday in order to get ready. Bud Ulrich was the referee, and he was joined by fellow Winnipeger Ken Lazaruk, with Bill Wright and Dave Barr from Edmonton, and Vancouverite Larry Rohan rounding out the crew.

Business was always the first order and because of the different time zones the crew decided to turn in early in order to be ready when the whistle blew. Shortly after they fell asleep, Ken was awakened by a loud banging on the wall separating them from the adjoining room. Recognizing the noise, he was confident that it would soon stop.

However the noise was relentless and continuous, fluctuating between an intense and rapid banging, and a slow measured thumping, but never stopping. Frustrated because he couldn't sleep, and no doubt jealous of the incredible staying power of the couple generating the sleep-depriving racket, he decided to take matters into his own hands.

Ken fumbled in the dark for his whistle, and placing it close to the wall, blew like hell. Immediately the banging stopped and for a few seconds was replaced with muffled giggling. There was no further disturbance and Ken returned to bed impressed with the newfound use for his whistle.

The next morning when he opened his hotel room door he ran smack into his next-door neighbour, a defensive back for the Western team. When the player heard the whistle he thought it was one of his coaches who he wasn't going to risk upsetting before the game with his continual banging on the walls. They immediately recognized each other and started to laugh. What a way to start the weekend. It should have been an omen of things to come.

The game went off without a hitch and the crew returned to the hotel for a quick meeting, facing the rare opportunity of spending an entire Saturday evening together out on the town.

As they discussed what local nights spots would be honored with their presence, there was a knock on the door. On the other side was a generous supply of beer from the game sponsor, which was welcomed with open arms, especially since game officials rarely shared in any game sponsor's generosity.

An hour later, with the supply now greatly diminished, there was another knock on the door. It was their next-door neighbour and a few of his teammates looking for their beer that had been sent to the wrong room. After disposing of the remaining suds, the players asked the officials to join them at the Elephant and Castle for the post-game festivities.

They didn't have to ask twice; besides it was free. During the season, officials rightfully avoid the players like the plague, but it was preseason and an official event, making it seem like a great idea, especially at the price. After several more hours of accumulated drinking and good times, discretion dictated it was time to move on, recognizing that familiarity breeds contempt.

Where to go? It was too early to go back to the hotel and they decided to absorb some of the local colour and headed for a waterfront bar, as their ability to make rational decisions was quickly being diminished. Larry Rohan, the only Vancouverite on the crew, knew the area well and reluctantly joined them because he was their sole source of transportation. They tried to get a table where they could keep their backs to the wall, but they were all taken. Instead, they settled for a table in the middle of the room where they alternated their attention between the dancer sliding down the pole, and the horseplay and joking around you expect from over-grown boys.

However there was a certain uneasiness at the table because of the menacing glances directed their way from two shabbily dressed Polish sailors, who sat at the adjacent table. The crew attempted to initiate a conversation, but it soon became evident that the two sailors, who remained stone-faced, knew as much English as the officiating crew knew Polish: absolutely none.

Lazaruk was an educator and decided to take over. He was bilingual, he could speak English, and English accompanied by sign language, which made him a natural as a referee later in his career. Ken was equally unsuccessful, even when he spoke more slowly and at the top of his voice, convinced it would solve the communication problems.

Finally Ken raised his glass and shouted the only two words he knew "Lech Walesa." The mood of the sailors was immediately transformed as they jumped to their feet and returned the toast. The sailors quickly joined the officials' party as they continued to toast each other, with neither party having the slightest idea of what their new lifetime friends were saying.

Larry, who had stopped drinking because he was driving, knew it was time to leave and dragged the reluctant crew from the bar. Over Larry's objections, the rest of the crew insisted on giving the sailors a ride back to the ship, and they all piled into Larry's oversized International Van that was more suitable for selling eggs and honey.

The sailors directed Larry along the darkened waterfront, motioning him to stop in front of a large ominous looking fishing trawler. It was reminiscent of the black and white 1930s movie where fog covered the waterfront and sailors were Shanghaied from local bars, thrown aboard a ship, never to see their families again.

As the sailors hit the pavement, they beckoned their new friends to come aboard. Larry, now the only official with operating brain cells, knew of the danger they faced and yelled, "Let's get out of here." However Ken, Bill and Dave were determined to "come aboard" and began to climb out of the van.

Art McAvoy, who was sitting next to Larry, was also scared, and there was no way he was going to get out of the van. Suddenly Bill Wright grabbed Art by the arm and tried to drag him from the van. Larry hit the gas peddle and Art was able to break Bill's death grip, leaving the three amigos alone in front of the ship.

They stood together decked out in their suits and ties, scanning the ship for the gangplank, but there was none. In fact the ship appeared entirely encased with a chain link fence topped with rusty barbed wire, which seemed in better shape than the ship. They were forced to crawl through a small hole in the fence, with no apparent damage to their fine threads. As they climbed aboard, the stench from the fish was irrepressible and when combined with all the liquor they had consumed, it invoked an almost uncontrollable urge to hurl their cookies.

The fivesome made its way down a narrow, poorly lit corridor, which even in the low light was not able to hide its neglect, to a small room with an even smaller table. The sailors quickly produced a bottle of vodka and five shot glasses, and it started all over again.

After five more Lech Walesas, Ken noticed a large world map on the wall and pointed to Vancouver, whereupon one of the sailors traced a route through the Panama Canal directly to Poland. Then they turned and exposed a sly grin.

The entourage continued deeper into the bowels of the ship to a small galley where Ken, Bill, and Dave were directed to sit in an old-fashioned '50s style restaurant booth, which looked like it had been reclaimed from the garbage dump.

Now silent, the two sailors stood over the cornered officials at one end of the table. Suddenly one of the two produced a long bladed knife and held it over his head in a menacing fashion.

Ken thought it was all over, "I knew they were going to slit my throat and steal my suit."

Bill Wright wasn't scared, claiming: "I had so much to drink I knew that when he stuck the knife in, I wouldn't feel a thing."

Almost as quickly the other sailor produced some Polish sausage and a tomato, which his partner quickly sliced, and the party resumed, the three amigos breathing a collective sigh of relief.

At a time unknown to the trio they were once again on land, and quickly noticed the sun, which was now fully exposed above the horizon. With no idea where they were they cautiously made their way along the waterfront, until they encountered a heavily secured industrial site. After some begging the security guard called them a cab.

Back at the hotel, they banged on Bud's door anxious to share their experience. Bud's wife Diane had accompanied him on the trip, and he had been spared the night's adventures. Wisely, Bud refused to open the door, and while Ken refused to take no for an answer, Bud called security, expressing concern about the strangers at his door.

Luckily for the trio Ken was able to produce a room key, just before they were thrown out of the hotel. Ken claims he's never drank that much in his life, and hopes he never will again, but it's a risk he'll have to take as long as he is an official.

9

Grey Cup, eh?

As I peeled off my uniform in the cramped Regina dressing room, which was starting to fill with water from the broken shower, I couldn't believe another season was over.

As I tried to keep my suit pants out of the water, Jim Lysack stopped by to invite us to a barbecue. But our thoughts were on the present. The war was over for another year and beer was being consumed with a mixture of satisfaction, relief and a sense of regret that we would not see each other for another six months. There was also that sense of expectation, particularly for those who had had a good season and were thinking about Grey Cup appointments.

1974 had been a great year for me. It was the year I knew I had arrived as a CFL official. The league must have thought so too, because for the past two years I had worked every playoff week doing both semi-final and final games, including Winnipeg, which quite frankly I could have done without. (Winnipeg felt the same way, claiming they never get a break when I officiate their games, and who knows, maybe they're right.)

As I watched Jimmy try to get the barbecue started, I knew he was largely responsible for my success in the last two years. In 1972 I was still struggling, convincing no one, including myself, that I was anything but a journeyman official. Whether by design or good luck I was assigned to work with Jim, or Lou, as he was called by his friends, for the 1973 and 1974 seasons.

Jim was as good as any field official I would ever work with, and as physically and mentally tough as any man that I have ever met. When there was trouble on or off the field, I always hoped Jimmy was close by.

He was one of the few officials who could work every position on the field and do a good job. The league even tried to make a referee out of him, a position which requires a different set of skills. Fortunately, Jim put a quick end to that experiment when, with the help of the officiating and stick crews, he gave Hamilton four tries from the one yard line before they scored.

Jim was a no-nonsense guy who you wanted as a friend, and for the next two years he pushed me, encouraged me, taught me, gave me shit, and more importantly, was there when I needed help. My motivation for success was simple; fail and I lose the respect of one of most respected officials of the league. My improvement was dramatic, and I finally knew that I could handle any situation. Jim and I had become good friends off the field as well, something that could not have happened without respect and trust for each other on the field.

Suddenly it was time to head to the airport. I hated to go, because it was the first time I had been completely relaxed in six months.

"Jim, I've got to get going. Would you call me a cab?" I said, hoping he would give me a ride, which he did.

As we piled into his 10-year-old, 400 horsepower battleship Oldsmobile, which in many ways reflected his personality, I tried to think of the right words to thank him for all his help during the past two years. As the car lumbered along one of the back roads around the airport I finally ventured my feelings. "Jim, I would like to thank you for..." but before I could finish, Jim interrupted.

"Neil, I really enjoyed working with you, and I think we did a real good job together and there is no reason why you can't do the Grey Cup next year."

My attempted thanks had turned into an endorsement for my officiating, not only from a respected official, but from a friend I had made for life. Undoubtedly, the beer added to the euphoria of Jim's comments, but I was determined to grab the Grey Cup ring in 1975, which is every official's dream.

Suddenly we were at the airport as Jim brought his beast to a halt in front of the Air Canada entrance. "You check in, while I grab your bags," he said, as he scrambled out of the driver's side. We had cut our arrival to the last-minute, and missing a flight out of Regina was not an option, because the next question to the agent was, what day is the next flight to Winnipeg?

Luckily, the flight had been delayed in Vancouver giving Jim and I plenty of time to head for the men's room and release some of the pressure. As we stood side-by-side enjoying the instant relief in the empty washroom, Jim produced a paper bag from his jacket. "What have you got there?" I asked as I looked around the room to make sure no one else was around. "It's homemade wine that you didn't have time to try," he whispered as he pushed the bag towards me.

I took a quick mouthful. It tasted like panther piss, but I quickly replied, "Not bad." Before Jim could put the bag back in his pocket an RCMP officer appeared and blocked our way out of the washroom. "What do you have in that bag?" he demanded, looking directly at us. We put our cards on the table and told him we were celebrating the end of the season.

We escaped with a warning to be more careful in what could have been a very embarrassing situation. Fortunately, for us, everyone in Saskatchewan happens to be a football fan.

I could hardly wait for the 1975 season to start. I had been waiting 15 years and I'd made up my mind that this is the year I was going to work the Grey Cup. I had just come off a great year, I had the experience, and I had finally figured out what officiating in the CFL was all about.

For the first time, I was actually looking forward to getting in shape. Gord Johnson, a fellow Winnipeg CFL official who I had worked with for the last 15 years in both amateur and pro, was also pushing for his first Grey Cup.

Gord and I start our physical conditioning program the same way every year. I was desperately trying to get the yard in shape, now that the snow had disappeared, knowing full well that within a couple of months, once the season had started, I would be lucky to have time for a haircut, when Gloria stuck her head of the door. "Neil, it's Gord on the phone," she yelled, resigning herself to the start of another season.

As usual, my conversation with Gord was brief, if not ritualistic. "Neil, it's Gord. How are you?"

"Fine," and after a slight pause, "Are you ready?"

Little did he know how ready I was when I responded in the usual affirmative, "Tomorrow night 6:30 at River East, don't be late." We both laughed; nothing further had to be said.

Like clockwork we both arrived together, Gord bouncing an old basketball, which quickly became the centre of our attention in a one-on-one match-up on the outside asphalt court. It didn't take long before a couple of high school kids would arrive with the same purpose in mind, but there was only one basket. Those summer evenings featured some great two-on-two confrontations between a number of high school kids and two old geezers, with the kids usually coming out on the short end of the score. Gord was very slight and turning grey, and the kids thought he was a pushover. There was no way I was going to tell the young bucks that Gord played for the Winnipeg Stellars, national basketball champions, as he blocked shot after shot.

But competing with these high school kids had its price, absorbing many elbows, bruises and blistered feet, which we agreed was a small price to pay to get in shape because Gord and I both hated running. What I didn't tell Gord was that every night we didn't play basketball I was out running my ass off doing wind sprints, looking for that little edge over the rest of the guys, including my good friend Gord. My previous training consisted of finding my shoes two weeks before the season started and trying them out at the local park to make sure they didn't hurt my feet. Now here I was bent over barfing my guts out doing wind sprints. This wasn't the Neil Payne I knew.

I was completely prepared when the season started, and it showed in my work. Baseball hitters, when they're in the groove, claim they can see the spin on the ball. I was in the same groove. I swear I could see Jake Gaudaur's signature on the ball, and everything was happening in slow motion. No matter what the situation, I was always in a good position for getting a good look, and more importantly making the right call. Things couldn't be better.

Wilkie was still driving us crazy drawing the defense offside, but if the referee didn't want to penalize him, then that was his problem. I just kept throwing the flags.

But this year we had a new problem. Bill Baker, the B.C. defensive end, affectionately referred to as "the undertaker" by all except the ball carriers he decapitated, had developed a new technique of clothes-lining backs as they ran through the line. It would be hilarious if it weren't so damn dangerous. Bill must have thought this one up watching Saturday morning cartoons, where the villain runs smack into the low hanging branch of a tree, and goes absolutely no further. I guarantee Bill's arm is as big as any at tree branch.

What made Bill so good was he never cocked or swung his arm, at least we never saw him. He simply stuck it out and destroyed all incoming traffic. In spite of a number of players getting their collective bells rung, we continued to argue whether his tactics were legal. Finally we got the word—unless we called him, there wouldn't be enough backs left to finish the year.

I got my chance and I watched the B.C. defensive line like a hawk, waiting for the dastardly deed. I couldn't believe that not only was it a clothes-line but he swung his arm as well. I was so excited I miss-fired before I finally threw my flag. Got him!

Shit, I realized, it wasn't Baker, only an imitator who had a lousy technique. I'm not sure we ever caught Bill, and just like Wilkie, he continued to drive us crazy. But I had more important things to worry about: that Grey Cup appointment.

Again I was assigned to work the final between Edmonton and Saskatchewan, and I was certain I was on my way to the Grey Cup. I'd had a great year and there were lots of hints that I'd be in Calgary for the big game.

The final was a bitterly cold Edmonton day, where you could see your breath even in the dressing room. The two teams hated each other, and tried to beat each other into submission. It was a Western classic.

The league still wouldn't let us use gloves or cover our ears and I couldn't stop shaking on the sideline. I'm not sure whether it was nerves, or whether I was slowly freezing to death.

The line play was particularly vicious as I stood on the sideline watching the yard between the offensive and defensive lines slowly disappear. Steam escaped from the holes in the linemen's helmets, which when coupled with the steam snorting from their noses that they directed at their opponents across line, made them look and sound like wild beasts trying to stake out their territory as they charged into each other.

The game was close when Saskatchewan decided to gamble on a crucial third down short-yard situation. "Hut, hut," and suddenly Ron Estay, the Edmonton defensive captain, sprung across the line before the ball was snapped. An easy call; I threw my flag.

I ran toward referee Don Barker, who was now surrounded by the team captains, including Estay, all waiting for my call. "Sir, I have Edmonton No. 55 offside." Suddenly Captain Estay was in my face demanding, "What did you call?"

I was looking into a face that was reserved for horror movies and Western finals. His face was covered with yellow- and red-coloured ice, which had formed with the mixture of blood and mucous that he was still snorting through his nose, a sight that was made more horrid by a pair of wild and enraged eyes that were looking right through me.

Again I repeated the penalty, but his piercing eyes never left me. In an obvious effort to control his rage he said, "Mr. Payne, if I wasn't a Christian gentleman, I would kill you." His voice was now quivering. I had no doubt about his sincerity, and it was the first time I had any appreciation of the qualities of born-again Christians.

What the hell happened, I wondered. Did I miss something? I ran back to my position on the sideline. Did the guard move, was I asleep, was the guard screened by the tackle? I had no idea, but Estay was certain I had blown the call.

The rest of the game appeared to go pretty well, but the offside call was uncomfortably stuck in the back of my mind. The day grew colder and colder, and finally the gun sounded, sending Edmonton off to the Grey Cup and the officials to our dressing room.

I could hardly wait, not only for the long anticipated Grey Cup appointment, but also for a chance to thaw out, hoping certain frozen members of my body wouldn't fall off in the process. The dressing room looked like a cheap strip tease show, as we pulled off layer after layer of underwear that we were able to squeeze under our pants and shirts. Even our stinky body heat was a welcome relief from the frigid cold. But as we all went through our post game ritual we were all thinking the same thing: who's working the Grey Cup?

It didn't take long before Hap walked through the dressing room door to announce the Western appointments. Hap was always in control, and demanded complete silence before making the announcement. Why not? I wanted to hear my name loud and clear. Just as every Canadian who ever put on a pair of pads dreamed about playing in the Grey Cup, I had that same burning desire to step on that field, and my time had finally come and I was going to savour every second.

Finally Hap took centre stage while we sat in our chairs awaiting his pronouncement. I fixed my eyes on the floor knowing my name would be the last to be called. Hap started "Referee Barker, Line Umpire Ferguson, and Field Judge Pilling."

No "Payne." What? I had a great year; why is he doing this to me?

My whole world came crashing down on the dressing room floor. I wanted to jump up and tell Hap to stick my whistle up his ass, but I was too stunned and hurt as my eyes remained fixed on the floor. I started jamming my equipment into my bag, carefully avoiding the eyes of my fellow officials because I was too embarrassed, and knowing I would likely say something I would regret or even worse, start crying. The atmosphere in the dressing room was tense and quiet but I knew when I wished the crew "good luck" and closed the door behind me, they'd be celebrating their Grey Cup appointments, which they deserved.

I just wanted to get on the airplane and go home. The Sunday night flight to Winnipeg was jammed as I fought my way to my window seat over the wing. My face was soon pressed against the window, and with my eyes fixed on the flashing lights at the end of the wing, I invited every negative emotion to pass through my body.

I felt guilty because I felt almost as bad the day my dad died, experiencing many of the same feelings. I felt cheated and hurt that something I wanted so badly had been taken from me, and complete despair that I was totally helpless to change what had happened.

"Sir, would you like chicken or beef?" the flight attendant asked, momentarily snapping me out of my trance. I replied with a hurt "Nothing," and she quickly moved on to the next row. Suddenly there was food all over the floor, which was quickly followed by the stewardess, who landed on her butt as the plane twisted through a series of wild gyrations. It was the first time I had heard people scream on an airplane.

Normally a white-knuckle flyer, I didn't even flinch. In fact I hoped the plane would crash and put me out of my misery, but with my luck I realized that I'd probably live and spend the rest of my life in a wheelchair. Could life get any worse?

Gloria, my life support, was waiting for me at the airport and she accentuated the positives of the year, which fell on deaf ears. The next morning my feelings hadn't changed, and I wrote my letter of resignation. Thankfully I followed the advice I had given to my own employees, and stuck it in my desk for a couple of weeks before sending it to the league.

My letter never got out of the drawer because, sure enough, I had missed a procedure when I called Edmonton offside, and even though I had a great year it was never more evident that you are only as good as your last call. The question in the league's mind still remained: was I good enough to do the big game?

For 15 years I had focused my total effort and energies on one thing; to work a Grey Cup, demanding many sacrifices from Gloria and the family. If I quit now, I know the question of whether I was good enough would haunt me for the rest of my life, and I knew I wouldn't have an answer.

Spring brought new hope and another season, where my Grey Cup chances appeared to evaporate even before the regular season started. Jim Lysack and I were reunited, which could only help my on-field performance, but our preseason bonding brought us nothing but trouble. We were scheduled to work our first preseason game in Vancouver on Wednesday and to return to Edmonton for a Saturday night game instead of going home between games.

Both Hap, who was in his last year as director, and Bill Fry, his successor, arrived from the East and came to watch the crew in our first two games, and evaluate Larry Rohan in his rookie debut. Our performance in the first game was as expected for the first game of the season—shaky. Bill and Hap were not pleased and told Jim and me that they would see us in Edmonton.

Bill and Hap left on an early Thursday morning flight for Edmonton. Jim and I weighed all our options and concluded that staying in Vancouver until Saturday had infinitely more possibilities.

We ran into Jim's brother and spent two incredible days painting the town red, only stopping when we ran out of paint.

Our early Saturday morning flight to Edmonton was delayed for over four hours because of mechanical problems, and when we arrived at the hotel in Edmonton we were already late for the team meeting. The rest of the crew, together with Bill and Hap, had already started the meeting when we tried unsuccessfully to explain why we were two days late.

Hap didn't care to listen, "Where in the heck have you guys been?" he shouted. "We've been sitting for two days waiting for you."

"Shit, I knew we should have told them we were staying in Vancouver." We were dead meat.

Hap, now totally enraged, vented his anger, which had been building for two days as he and Bill sat in the hotel room waiting for us to arrive. There was no place to hide. We had dug ourselves a deep hole, and the season hadn't even started. I knew any chance of working the

Grey Cup was gone. I wasn't one of Hap's favourite boys because he thought I had too much fun off the field, and I had just proven him right.

The lecture was far from over, and once we got to the park, Syd Bercov, who was our referee and crew chief, gave us hell about not being prepared and demanded that we hustle our butts off all night. The message had been delivered. The atmosphere in addressing room was one usually reserved for the playoffs, with each official carrying out his duties in deadly silence, which included blowing up the balls, measuring the length of the yardsticks, or anything else we could find to convince Bill and Hap that we were ready.

When they finally left dressing room, we began to put the finishing touches on getting dressed. "Shit," Syd blurted out, his face turning white. "I forgot my short-sleeved shirt," a mandatory league requirement. We tried cutting his sleeves off, but finally settled for pinning them up under his armpits.

Our dressing room location required that we cross the field to get to our positions on the sideline for the anthem. As we stood in the doorway behind Syd, he turned and looked us in the eye and in a commanding voice demanded, "We're going to sprint across that field and show Hap we're ready." I couldn't believe it. Syd was his own man—had management finally got to him? Syd might hustle during a play but would never run when walking would do, and running before a game was out of the question.

But here we were sprinting across the field, Syd in the lead, with the crew tightly in tow. Suddenly Syd applied the brakes, and resumed his usual saunter, as the rest of us piled into him like the keystone cops. He mumbled something about running only when it was important, and we knew we had our leader back.

As expected, the crew did an excellent job, particularly the two high fliers from Vancouver, which was a perfect way to end the preseason. Hap's concern was our performance on the field, and he was happy with our night's work. But the main purpose of his trip was to watch Larry perform in his first two games, which had turned into a four-day ordeal.

Hap had one final task. He opened his notebook in which he made notes during the last two games that were intended to get Larry ready for the season opener. Like the rest of us, even though he was still a rookie, Larry was strong willed and opinionated and carried the additional burden of being a prototype American who knew everything.

Hap offered Larry any number of suggestions on how to improve his positioning, movement, and other constructive advice that any rookie would be happy to receive. But no, not Larry. He challenged, rebutted and disagreed with everything Hap said before someone told him to shut up. But it was too late.

Exasperated by the week's activities, Hap understandably came apart and wanted to fire Larry on the spot. In spite of the crew's problems, Syd convinced Hap to give Larry another chance. Twenty-five years later, Larry is still a pain in the ass, albeit a lovable one.

As I packed my bag I realized the only way I was going to the Grey Cup was if I phoned the league office and bought a ticket.

I worked just as hard as I had the previous year, but I was enjoying it more. I had to; I was even better, there were no questionable calls, no self-doubt, and my sometimes shaky confidence was being replaced with a growing arrogance, something I hated in other officials, but quickly discarded after a one-way conversation with Jim Lysack.

In spite of the preseason problems, I knew I would get a chance at a playoff game, because I had too good a year to ignore. When I received the call to do the semifinal, I wasn't surprised but I was a little disappointed because I knew I probably wouldn't get the finals. But a week later, I was off again to do the Western final. The stage was set once again, only this time it was even colder, with the exhaust fumes from the cars hanging around the stadium looking for a way to get in to watch the game.

My thoughts of last year's disappointment were interrupted by the five-minute buzzer. Forget about the Grey Cup and everyone else, I thought; work your ass off and take whatever happens.

I couldn't believe it: Bill Fry told us we could wear gloves for the first time, and I actually felt warm at the opening whistle, although my runny nose told me winter had arrived.

We were underway and my mind wouldn't leave me alone. Watch the offside, watch the tackle, count the players, put up the gates, watch the late hits, no cheap flags...

Suddenly, Edmonton fumbled the ball. It came right at me followed by a horde of players from both teams, who were trying desperately, but unsuccessfully, to recover the frozen ball. Just before it hit the sideline, I saw an arm with a green sleeve protrude from the mass of players and touch it. If the play had happened in July with everyone wearing short sleeve shirts I would have had absolutely no idea who touched the ball last. I quickly signaled Saskatchewan ball, which turned out to be one of the crucial plays of the game.

I kept pushing, play after play, knowing there would be one or two plays that would impact the outcome of the game, hoping that I would be the official covering them and I wasn't disappointed. There were several crucial sideline judgments involving passes caught right on the sideline where I was fortunate enough to be in perfect position to make the calls.

It was a game that I didn't want to end, but when the final gun sounded I was physically and mentally spent, but I had finally answered the question. Yes, I could handle the big game. I had satisfied the most severe critic of all: myself.

I savoured every step back to the dressing room, knowing I had nothing else to give. As I expected, the film review showed it was probably the best game that I had ever worked. The post game in the dressing room was a replay of the previous year. Hap had sent Bill to announce the crew, no doubt having more than he could stomach of western officials for one-year, particularly Payne and Lysack.

Again, Bill, in his usual well-orchestrated post-game meeting, held everyone in suspense, hanging on his every word, waiting for his pronouncement as he scanned the silent room. "The crew for the Grey Cup is as follows: Referee Don Barker (no surprise—Don's the best referee around and it's the west's turn), Umpire Bill Dell (shit, I hoped Jim would go, but after Vancouver, not a chance), Back Umpire John Stroppa (great choice, lucky John gets to do his first Cup), Head Linesman Jacques Decarie (hell, another rookie, now I'm jealous), and finally, Field Judge, doing his first Grey Cup, Neil Payne." After 15 years of struggling, waiting, and too many disappointments, it had finally happened. I was going to the Grey Cup.

I was close to tears, but there was no time. Jim Lysack was in my face crushing my right hand with his vice-like grip. I wanted to hug him but wouldn't dare because he was liable to smack me in the head. He looked me in the eye and said, "No one deserves it more, partner. You'll do great job."

Nothing further had to be said.

Our early season bonding in Vancouver paid off, in spite of almost being fired. Pro sports, whether you're a player or an official, is all about performance on the field, and the job we did was just too good to ignore.

Just like after last year's final, I could hardly wait to get home, only for entirely different reasons. I wanted to share my happiness with Gloria, because she was the one that made all the sacrifices so her boy could go out and play. The regular weekly washing and meticulous pressing and packing of my uniform and equipment; the challenge of finding my airline ticket, which had I left a new hiding place that I could no longer recall; going alone to family functions; and unsuccessfully trying to contact me, when, as my daughter Heather would say, I was on cloud nine, my favourite hang out; encouraging me when I really needed a kick in the pants; and worse, being alone every weekend with four kids when even escape to the local supermarket only brought abuse from people she didn't know for calls I didn't make. She had done it all, while I, selfishly, all too often took her for granted.

I could hardly wait for the plane to land to share my incredible feelings with the entire family, which was common practice for all of us no matter what the situation. It hurt that my biggest fan, my father, wouldn't be there. He had died suddenly four years earlier before seeing what he wouldn't have believed possible, his son working the Grey Cup. I couldn't forget him telling me, "Remember, nothing either good or bad lasts forever," which was tailor-made to describe my fortunes in the last two years.

Gloria was parked in front of the terminal and when I opened the car door to tell her the news, I was too late. It was written all over my face. Thanking her for all her sacrifices wasn't good enough. "How would you like to go to the Grey Cup?" I proudly asked

"As much as I would like to, this is your time. You deserve it, go and enjoy it," she said. It was the same answer I would hear three more times when I got appointed to future Cups. Gloria must have known the future because when I became a supervisor she attended more Grey Cups than anyone could handle, and enjoyed every minute.

For the next two days, the phone never stopped ringing, with everyone offering congratulations. Relatives who had given up hope that I'd ever get the game, local amateur officials who knew the rocky road of being an official, and even the local media wanting to talk to the rookie about his first Cup. I was in my glory, lots of attention, and my mind was everywhere but on the upcoming game.

Wednesday morning, and it was time to pack and head for Toronto. As I looked at my carefully pressed uniform that Gloria once again neatly arranged on the bed, it hit me. I had a game to do. I had seen all too often teams that had gotten to the big game and were just happy to be there, and cheated both their fans and themselves.

The two things I valued and protected most as an official were my pride and my reputation, and I knew they would force me to do the best job I could. Besides, I had worked too hard too long to do anything else; at least that's what I told myself.

Wednesday and Thursday in Toronto did nothing to get the crew ready for the game. We attended all the functions, including the Schenley Awards, but thankfully we couldn't find the Calgary pancake breakfast, because we had already enjoyed far too many of the Grey Cup festivities. Friday morning Hap wisely took us out to the stadium to work out, and the reality of why we were there hit home. The fun was over and I could feel the nerves starting to take over. The crew spent all of its time together. Bill Dell and I had not worked together since the officiating debacle in Winnipeg in 1970, and while we never discussed it, I knew we were both determined to show each other that we were both capable of doing a much better job.

When we gathered for our Saturday after-lunch meeting, I was developing a sore throat and couldn't eat. The crew was concerned that I was coming down with the flu. Bill, who looked after everyone, asked, "Neil, can we find you a doctor?"

"No, I'll be all right," I replied, knowing full well my condition had nothing to do with the flu. My body was now being controlled by pre-game jitters.

My lack of appetite was a blessing to Floyd Cooper, our standby official, who was consuming absolutely everything in sight, including my barely touched meal. Floyd had put his eating talents on display early in the week, and never ceased to amaze us with what seemed to be an ever-growing capacity to clear the table.

We constantly tried to scare Floyd, reminding him that he would be forced to go on the field if one of us got hurt, but to no avail. We all knew the chances of Floyd working were nonexistent.

By Saturday night I had a full case of the nerves. We were staying at the well-worn Royal York Hotel and Jacques Decarie and I were room-ing together. As rookies, we had naturally drawn a room next to the elevators. I knew sleep would be a problem but still decided to turn in early. It wasn't long before my body began to twitch and twist even though my head remained firmly fixed on the pillow. Shortly thereafter, my body began dancing to the continuous ding, ding, ding of the pass-ing elevators. Even when the elevators stopped, my mind had no trou-ble reproducing their aggravating sounds. Sleep was impossible, and I decided to go downstairs and get some fresh air, and take in the legen-dary Grey Cup activities that had been taking place in the lobby ever since a group of Calgarians rode their horses through it in 1948.

I pushed my way outside and took a slow walk around the block. The cool air felt good. When I got back to the hotel, people were lined up outside the main entrance, trying unsuccessfully to push their way past security. Now I couldn't even get in the hotel, never mind get to sleep.

I finally battled my way into the lobby with the elevators of course located at the far end. It was a scary sight, people wedged solidly to-gether pushing and yelling, having a great time with glasses raised over their heads so they wouldn't spill their valuable cargo. If anyone had fallen, there would have been no getting up until the next morning when the cleaning staff scraped them off the floor.

I inched my way to the elevator only to hear the security guard say, "Sorry sir, the elevators aren't working."

"How in the hell do I get to my room?" I asked. He pointed to the stairs where another mob of people was trying to push up the stairs past a couple of over-matched security guards.

Over an hour later, now exhausted, I completed my journey. I hit the pillow and I was gone.

In spite of my fears, the sun did come up the next morning. I was glad that the game had an early start so I did not have much time to worry.

I couldn't believe it. There I was tying my shoes, something I had done a thousand times before in Pee Wee, Bantam, Midget, high school, Junior, College, and CFL games, but never at a Grey Cup game. At that point, my nerves were starting to win the war and I knew I had to get them under control.

My thoughts were interrupted by the sound of the five-minute warning buzzer, a sound that was different in every stadium, but they all sang the same tune; the moment of truth had arrived. My nervousness started to disappear, or at least that's what I tried to convince myself, but I would only truly know when I hit the field. Don Barker stood in the doorway getting prepared to marshal his squad. "Okay boys, just relax and let's go and do a good job," he said. Easy for him to say—this was his seventh Grey Cup.

When we hit the field, any nervousness that was left was replaced with pure adrenaline, injected by the atmosphere of the crowd and the importance of an event that brought the whole country together.

The crew formed a straight line near centre field for the anthem. We were surrounded by Canadian and provincial flags and the rest of the field was covered with bands and schoolchildren who were all part of the ceremonies. *Oh Canada* rang through the stadium. For a moment I forgot that I was an official, but I knew what it meant to be a Canadian.

I had never been that pumped in my life. Finally the field was cleared and we were ready for the opening kickoff. Hustle your butt off downfield and cover, get in the game, I told myself, but my commands were not required. I was so charged, I beat the kicking team downfield and I was so close that I could have made the tackle. I was miles away from where I should have been. Settle down, I thought, you're supposed to be under control. It was the players' job to get hyped.

It wasn't long before I had an offside call. I was still hyper as hell, but my focus was incredibly sharp and I was seeing things that I haven't seen all year, which isn't always good news for an official.

I had another flag and quickly ran toward Don to report, "Sir, I have offense No. 62 holding."

Don's puzzled look spoke volumes. I knew exactly what he was thinking. Sidemen don't call holding on the offensive line, and he was right. I was so totally focused that I had reacted immediately to what I had seen without any further evaluation, which can eventually spell the kiss of death for any official.

It was a wake-up call. By time I got back to the sideline, I was in total control of my emotions and I knew the rest would be easy. The holding penalty turned out to be an excellent call, as a defensive end was tackled just as he attempted to get the quarterback. But it was time to worry about my own responsibilities, not everyone else's.

Prior to the game, no doubt in an effort to calm the rookie's nerves, Don Barker told me "The Grey Cup is the easiest game of the year to work." He was right. The teams were afraid to make a mistake and stayed away from penalties. Even the benches were quiet. Just like us, they were focused on the game and didn't have time to bitch about missed calls, real or imagined.

Don Barker stood at centre field and with three toots on his whistle signaled three minutes left in the first half. We got together for a pep talk during the time out. It was the first chance I had to look at the clock, which convinced me that indeed there were only a few minutes to play in the first half, even though it seemed the game had just started. As we stood together waiting for the end of the time out, knowing I was having a good game, I finally realized that the 15 years, with all their disappointments and detours, had been well worth the price. It couldn't get any better. Even the game was a classic, with both Saskatchewan and Ottawa taking turns in controlling the play.

I hustled back to my spot on the sidelines, reminding myself yet again: stay in the game; it's almost half time. Tony Gabriel, the all-star Ottawa receiver and their go-to guy, was flanked to my side. At the snap, he took off down the sideline. I was right behind him when the pass hit him in the hands.

Suddenly, I had no place to go. And then, bang!

I heard a voice say: "Neil, are you okay?"

Shit, I thought, what am I doing laying on the ground? All I could see was a forest of legs blocking my view. I must have been in dreamland for a while, because my rear end was soaking wet from lying on the field. I finally got to my feet, but after what I'd been through there was no way I was not going to finish the game.

One slight problem. I had a monster headache that would make a hangover seem like a welcome relief. John Stroppa found my hat, which he placed back on my head, but as I looked for my metal finger whistle, all I could find was the ring that once held the whistle. I had been hit so hard that the weld holding the whistle to the ring had snapped.

I tried to locate the broken piece of the whistle. Finally Ron Lancaster, the Saskatchewan quarterback, stepped in and said, "Neil, it's almost halftime, why don't you go the dressing room and get ready for the second half." What a brilliant idea, particularly since I didn't have a whistle. Hell, I had been in the league for seven years and it was the first time he'd ever spoke to me. I didn't even think he knew my name.

As I made my way across the field, my mind had almost fully cleared, but every step reminded me of my aching head. Bill Dell helped me off the field and we made our way past Floyd Cooper, who was now half frozen, sitting in a chair at the timer's bench watching the game.

Bill recalls, "We had a tough time getting Floyd out of the chair. He wanted no part of going onto the field."

I don't know why—he should have had enough protection against the weather from all the food he had consumed during the week. I had no idea what happened and it wasn't until the next day when I read Jack Matheson's column in the *Tribune* that I found out that I was hit by both Tony Gabriel and Ted Provost from Saskatchewan. Thank God it took two! I'd hate to spend the next 25 years trying to explain how I was knocked out by one lousy football player.

At halftime George Black, who was still an amateur official, ran with me up and down the sidelines to see if I could handle going back in. But my head still pounded with every step. For selfish reasons I wanted to finish the game, but I knew that Floyd, who was now warm and ready to go, would be a lot sharper than me in my present condition. So it was decided he would finish what I couldn't.

Hap suggested that I watch the second half from Floyd Cooper's chair at the timer's bench at field level. I frantically looked for Jacques' toque to keep me warm while the crew left the dressing room for the second half. Alone, the emotions of the pressures of the week came together with the realization that after 15 years of struggle I came up short... I broke down. Totally dejected, I plunked myself down in Floyd's chair next to Deke McBrien, the game's time-keeper. The toque made me look more like a lost soul than the injured official the CBC kept flashing throughout the game from a cameraman who had taken up permanent residence next to me at the timer's bench.

The timing crew tried to help and repeatedly asked if there were anything I needed. Jokingly I replied, "Sure would be nice to have something to drink." Deke quickly bent over and produced a brown paper bag from under the timer's table. Before he could go any further I frantically interjected, "No, I was just kidding." I could just imagine the reaction when CBC showed the injured official drinking from a paper bag at the timer's bench. Although the CFL fans reaction would have been predictable. "Eh, man, no problem it's Grey Cup," I still have no idea what was in that bag, but my guess is it was reflective of the Grey Cup spirit.

From my seat I watched one of the Grey Cup classics, with Ottawa winning in the last few seconds on a Clements-to-Gabriel pass. The atmosphere in the officials' dressing room was euphoric, generated by the final release of all the pressures of the season, and the knowledge that the crew had done a good job, feelings that can only be shared between officials who were between the lines.

Unfortunately I would have to wait even longer to share that experience.

As with any typical male, I called home looking for sympathy, and using my newly found injured voice asked "Gloria, did you watch the game?"

After several seconds hesitation she replied, "I watched the beginning," meaning she watched the introductions to make sure I hadn't wrinkled my uniform. "You looked real good." She had no idea what happened, because she was too busy sewing the kids' clothes for Christmas. Did anyone care?

I firmly believe that everything happens for a reason, and the 1977 season offered ample proof. I was having a great year, but as desperately as I wanted another shot at the Cup, I knew my chances were, at best, remote. Rarely did the league use the same official two years in a row, and besides Merv Pilling, my main competition who had replaced me in 1975 when I missed the call, was having a good year.

But fate stepped in on a crucial late season game in B.C., where Merv was almost a yard out in marking an out of bounds play, which normally goes unnoticed, but in this case was crucial. It cost B.C. a first down and the game, and Merv a Grey Cup appointment. He had returned my 1975 favour and opened the door for me to go back to the Grey Cup.

My playoff performance was even better than the regular season. I was fortunate enough to make a crucial pass interference call downfield in the Western final when the field judge was on the other side and couldn't get back in time to cover. I was off to the Grey Cup again, this time in Montreal.

I had worked both the semi and final games in the West. The Winnipeg and British Columbia semi-final was a heart-stopping game, a typical Western playoff with B.C. beating Winnipeg 33 to 32 with the usual last-minute heroics. It was also a miserable cold day, and the rain never relented. By the final gun I was totally soaked, and water continued to drip from the peak of my hat, yet as I headed for the dressing room, I felt satisfied that the teams determined the outcome of the game.

Gord Paterson, Winnipeg's homegrown all-star receiver, blocked my way to the dressing room and was quickly in my face. Gord and I had known each other for 10 years as we ran parallel paths, he as a player, me as an official. I had worked his games through his amateur and professional career, and we were both trying to get to the same place, the Grey Cup.

"Neil that's the worst fucking officiating I've ever seen. You guys are rotten, and cost us the game." Again I was the benefactor of those so-called intangible benefits of working your home team.

Gord, who at times was a pain in the butt, was also a very intense competitor and the frustration of not going to the big game came tumbling out. I knew exactly how he felt; I'd been there.

Not only had Merv given me the chance to go to Montreal to work at Olympic Stadium in front of 68,000 fans, the largest crowd ever at a Grey Cup, but even better, I was going with Jim Lysack, who also was assigned to do the game, and without his help I'd probably have watched it back home on TV.

When I landed in Montreal Wednesday night, I ran into Don Barker, our standby referee, at the airport. When we hit the hotel lobby Jimmy was already waiting. He'd come in a day early and the country kid from Regina was anxious to share the amazing discoveries he had made in the big French city.

Within minutes, the three Musketeers were heading down the street in anticipation of Jim's new discoveries. Jim ushered us into a nearly empty pub, and he immediately flashed three fingers at the bartender. Tray in hand the bartender produced three quart size bottles of Molson's finest product. Jim was truly impressed and excited about his discovery. "Aren't these quart bottles great! Just think—we won't have to spend all our time ordering more beer."

After finishing with Mr. Molson's product, there wasn't much time left to get to the Schenley Awards as we hustled back down the street. "What's your other discovery, Jim?" Don asked, this time with less enthusiasm. "I'm not telling you until after the Schenleys," he replied, still maintaining his excitement. We would have to wait.

Soon after the Schenleys had finished the entire crew, containing a mix of Eastern and Western officials, headed south, marching down Crescent Street right behind Jimmy in search of his second discovery. After the first one we could hardly wait.

We paraded down Crescent Street passing fully occupied bars and restaurants that were bubbling with activity. Jimmy made a quick turn and we followed him up a flight of stairs to again what appeared to be a near empty bar, probably one of the few in town. But it was too difficult to tell because the only light was flashing in our eyes.

"What do you think?" he demanded, as we looked quizzically at each other. "Have you ever seen this many breasts in your life?"

The entire bar was covered with plastic molded breasts, the ceiling, the walls, the bar, even the chairs. The only ones that weren't plastic belonged to the sole waitress, and even then I'm not so sure.

The laughter and howling were unanimous, and while a couple of guys were ready to leave, Jimmy insisted we stay for one drink, the most difficult part of which was trying to find a comfortable spot on the size 36D chairs.

It wasn't long before the Eastern and Western officials, who had never worked together before, broke down all of the imaginary barriers and we were talking about coverage and mechanics for Sunday's game. When Jimmy led us into the bar, we were a bunch of individual officials from all over the county. When we left, we were a crew, ready to step onto the field.

The long wait between Wednesday and the game on Sunday could be interminable, but I was determined to enjoy the atmosphere and the festivities. After all, I was a veteran who had worked last year's game— well, at least part of it, a fact that was still stuck uncomfortably in the back of my mind.

Jimmy and I went for a long walk Saturday morning and decided to stop at the Bonaventure for lunch and soak up some of the atmosphere. The restaurant was jammed with a small number of locals, who were engulfed by Grey Cup fans decked out in their team colours, together with the usual number of sports celebrities, who always drew a crowd.

As we sat down, Jimmy exchanged waves with Ron Lancaster, who was sitting on the other side of the room with a bunch of other players.

Now a CFL icon, Ron was having a great time not worrying about the pressure of Sunday's big game, since he had lost to Edmonton in the Western final.

Ron yelled at our table, "Neil, how are you feeling after last year's game?" As people stopped to hear what he had to say, I mumbled something about being "fine" while nodding my head up and down. He wasn't finished. "Neil, I was a little disappointed in you when you got hurt."

What the hell is he talking about, I wondered. But he wasn't finished "When I asked you how you were feeling, you said fine, but how's the crowd taking it?"

Not only was it a perfect shot, but everyone within range was laughing. Before he left, he wished us good luck on Sunday and we knew he meant it.

What about the game? There's not much to remember, which means the crew must have done a good job. The game was over early as Montreal bombed Edmonton 41 to 6.

For most of the game, Edmonton players and the officials spent their time trying to stay erect on an icy field that had been covered with chemicals to melt the ice, which only worsened the condition, while we watched the Montreal players zip back and forth with staple-covered shoes, another CFL winter tradition.

The only incident came late in the game when the crew apparently missed a clip on a meaningless Montreal touchdown, but even that turned out to be a blessing because the league finally realized it was impossible to provide adequate officiating with only five-men crews, and in 1978 they added another man on the field.

I had heard the final whistle before, but never with the same feeling. Finally, after 16 years, I got it done. I never even noticed the 68,000 fans who were celebrating their hometown win as I hustled through the tunnel to our dressing room, where I had my own celebrating to do.

Surprisingly, there was no laughing and back slapping. I didn't even want a beer because it might dull what I was feeling. I sat in my chair peeling off my equipment, finishing the journey I had started 16 years earlier. It was a feeling that is impossible to explain.

I had nothing further to prove to anyone, and more importantly to myself; although I knew I wasn't going to be totally satisfied until I was the referee.

Yet even that weekend wasn't without its disappointment. When I booked my return flight, I made sure I got out on Sunday night, believing the City of Winnipeg would come to a grinding halt if I wasn't at work on Monday morning. What a mistake.

We had returned to the hotel and Don, Jimmy and I were enjoying the satisfaction of doing a good job together. It was a special time for Jim, and I was considering all the games we had worked together and yes, by now the beer was flowing. It was time to go to the airport, but I didn't want to go, and tried frantically but unsuccessfully to change my flight. Don Barker didn't want the party to end either, and hid my suitcase. Regrettably it was soon found, and I was on my way to the airport missing out on what was fast becoming the most enjoyable night of my life.

I shouldn't have been surprised, because it was truly reflective of the story of my life. When something good happened to me, it usually didn't last for long, or if it did, I took it for granted, or was in too much of a damn hurry to enjoy it.

10

Where are the Broads?

It was 1976. Another season had begun, and we had just finished our first preseason game in Winnipeg on a beautiful prairie summer evening.

Among the crew was Ken Lazaruk, a Winnipeg amateur official, who with the guidance of all the veterans had just officiated his first game in the league. Both of Lazaruk's feet were still off the ground as we made our way through the tunnel from our dressing room to the world outside. He was feeling relieved that he had made it through his first game without screwing anything up.

As we opened the door at the other end, we encountered a group of a dozen or more young women who all seemed to possess the same attributes: sculptured bodies generously exposed by minimal wardrobes, which were also ideally suited for the warm evening. In a word, they were gorgeous.

The rookie's eyes began to grow, "Are they waiting for us?" he asked in a hopeful tone. I knew someone at the officiating school had told Ken, along with other tales, about all the women who hang around our dressing rooms.

"Ken, if all the women are waiting outside our door it means only one thing," I replied.

"What's that?" he asked, his eyes never leaving the girls.

"It means that the players dressing room is right next to ours and these girls are waiting for the players." His world was shattered, but better now because officials and women don't mix, with the women possessing a sixth sense that manages to keep them at a safe distance. Hell, even the hookers ignored us.

In my rookie years in the early '70s I used to enjoy going to Vancouver where the streets and bars were alive with nighttime activity, including numerous ladies of the evening who were incredibly young and beautiful for such a distasteful profession.

After a few trips I noticed that although the young women went boldly from one potential customer to another, not only did they totally ignore the officiating crew when we returned to our hotel after our post-game meal, they even turned their backs when we got close.

Finally the curiosity was too much, and I confronted one of the girls who continually ignored us. "Why won't you talk to us?" I asked.

"You know damn well why," she said, becoming defensive.

"I have no idea," I said, still looking for an explanation.

"You're Vancouver vice!" she shot back.

Still pressing, I asked, "What makes you think we're Vancouver vice?"

"Who else has those stupid brush cuts, and wears ugly suits and ties this late at night?" I told her football officials, but she was a non-believer. We couldn't even get lucky with the street girls.

One more encounter with the ladies of the evening cured me for good. Again we had just returned from a late-night meal when a car pulled up to the curb. I thought it was someone looking for directions, but when I looked through the passenger window I knew it was girls looking for paying company, and I couldn't resist asking for the price. "Eighty dollars for anything you want," she offered.

"That's too bad. I only have forty dollars," I replied, knowing the price was negotiable but that forty dollars wouldn't close the deal.

I turned away to join the guys. "Just a minute," she said as I turned back to hear her latest offer. "Forty dollars for straight sex," she said, agreeing to what I thought were ridiculous terms.

Looking for a graceful way to withdraw, I said, "That forty dollars, of course, includes the whole crew," pointing to the guys standing on the sidewalk. Her driver, who was even better looking, leaned over and shouted some well-known obscenities in my direction before speeding off into the night, but not before she had carefully run over my foot with the rear wheel of the car.

Thankfully, nothing was broken and the game was over because there was no way I could have worked the next day. I wonder how I would have explained to Hap that I was injured because some hooker ran over my foot. I was finally convinced that officials and women don't mix, particularly ladies of the evening.

I had just become a referee and was assigned to do the Sunday afternoon game in Ottawa in late October. I was grumbling about leaving the warmth of my chair to catch a late Saturday night flight for the game, because winter had come early to Winnipeg. I was reminded that those who think Portage and Main is the coldest spot in Canada have never taken the long walk from the parking lot to the terminal at the Winnipeg airport. There was no waiting because there were more agents than passengers, and it seemed the only ones who traveled Saturday night were officials and seniors looking for cheap fares.

I quickly headed for the restaurant and a cup of coffee to warm up before heading to the gate, passing a couple of cleaning staff who were washing the floor not because it needed it, but because they were bored.

Before I could sit down I spotted Bud Ulrich, another Winnipeg referee, who was on his way to Calgary. Immediately my mood changed. Our assignments were taking us to different ends of the country, but I hadn't seen Bud for months and it was a time to catch up on things.

We didn't have much time, but we were able to replay all our trials and tribulations that occurred in the previous month, stopping regularly to ensure there was enough time to laugh at things that didn't seem to be so funny when they first happened.

Even though the restaurant was nearly empty a young woman in her early 20s dressed in a smartly tailored suit, more suited to Wall Street than Winnipeg International, sat down directly in front of us. Undaunted we continued our conversation, but we soon became aware that the girl with the pleasant face was staring at us, listening to our every word.

Finally, Bud and I had to hustle down the corridor leading to the gates. It was time to part company and we wished each other good luck, which up until now wasn't needed because we were both having good years. As I headed for the gate I could hear the fast closing approach of high-heeled shoes on the marble floors. By the time I reached the gate I was joined by the young woman from the restaurant. I handed my ticket to the agent at the gate who asked, "Are you two travelling together?"

Before I could find an answer she responded, "Yes, we'd like to sit together."

My ego grew even larger.

The flight, like the airport, was almost empty. You would have been hard pressed to find enough bodies to fill a football team, although there was a friendly old timer and his wife who sat directly across from us.

The wheels weren't off the ground when my new friend was looking for complementary drinks, and doubles at that. "Won't you join me?" she asked. I thought it was easier to tell her I didn't drink than try and explain why officials don't drink before games. With each sip of her drink she became increasingly friendly. "Ever wonder what it's like to join the mile high club?" she asked.

I heard the question but wanted to make sure, "Pardon me?" I asked.

"Don't you wonder what it's like to get screwed on an airplane?" We both laughed as I quickly changed the subject.

After another drink, she turned to me and said, "Let's do it." I knew exactly what she meant.

"I'll go to the washroom in the back, then you follow me," she said. I turned to look at the washroom, then back at her, while thinking about the wife and kids back home.

"The timing isn't right," I said. "Maybe another time on another flight."

What I didn't tell you was that this sharply dressed, pleasant woman was big enough to be Chris Walby's twin sister, and I knew if both of us went into that undersized washroom, only one of us was coming out alive, and it wasn't going to be me.

Thankfully, dinner arrived. The seniors across the aisle knew exactly what was happening and strained to hear her every word. The old guy pretended he was reading the Air Canada magazine but he hadn't changed a page for over 20 minutes.

Nothing like a full stomach to curb our sexual desires? Wrong. Nonchalantly, she turned towards me and said, "I wish I had a box of popcorn," as she stared at the fly of my pants.

I could only guess where she was going, but I wasn't going to take the bait.

Even the flight attendant knew what was going on, and got into the act by politely asking, "Sir, can I get you a blanket?" Completely flustered, I headed for the washroom, checking several times to make sure the door was still locked behind me.

Years later, I still haven't joined the club even though I made an invitation to my wife on our flight to Hawaii. It was met by the expected reply: "Are you crazy?"

I thought she knew.

For unknown reasons, trips to Ottawa seemed to hold out some special adventure. In 1978, the league was looking for ways to improve the level of officiating. The officiating department convinced the Board of Governors that officiating would dramatically improve if entire crews traveled between east and west, something that had never been done before, since it was rather an expensive proposition when you started moving people between Montreal and Vancouver.

The heat was on. We had to produce. The first scheduled game for the traveling crew was a nationally televised mid-week game in Ottawa in early August, and we knew the crew that drew that game would be faced with additional media and league scrutiny.

My monthly appointments arrived by mail and were opened with the usual anticipation. I couldn't believe it. My crew was assigned to do the Ottawa game. It came as a shock because I was a rookie referee, and with the exception of Jim Lysak, who held the crew together, the rest of the guys were either working in new positions, or were relatively new officials.

What made it more surprising was that everyone told us we were the fourth-rated crew in the league, which isn't bad if there are ten crews, but there were only four. But our crew of so-called leftovers was doing a far better job than any one ever expected, and I was convinced that we could do the job.

Bill Fry made sure we arrived early at the hotel so we could have a special meeting before the big game. We stayed at the Lord Elgin, another officials' five-star hotel. I'm sure the Elgin was designed by a medieval architect, and the only difference between the rooms and the closets was that the closets had hangers.

It was a typical hot, muggy, Eastern day, something most of the Western officials had never experienced. Seven of us tried to squeeze into my room for our meeting, a physical impossibility. Ingenuity took over and three of us stayed in the room while Jim stood in the doorway and relayed Bills messages to the guys in the hall. The humidity was unbearable and everyone's white shirt stuck to their body like a wet T-shirt contest.

Bill delivered the message in his opening sentence. "Gentleman, this is the most important game of the year."

I knew he had forgotten the significance of the game when he assigned the crew.

"What did he say?" came from a voice in the hall. Bill and Jimmy tried to repeat the message at the same time. The rest was all downhill. If you asked the officials in the hall to compare notes with those who were in the room, I guarantee they would've thought they were at different meetings.

It wasn't long before a subhuman odor permeated the room, and evacuation was required for survival, bringing a merciful halt to the proceedings. Nothing more had to be said. Bill's presence had delivered the message.

I made sure we arrived at the park early. For a number of us on the crew, it was a chance to show we could handle new positions, for others a chance to show they belonged. By game time we were ready, and didn't wait for the customary five-minute warning before we hit the field. We mulled around, up and down the sideline, each of us getting ready for the extra scrutiny, while trying to deal with the heat and humidity.

"Neil," someone yelled. I turned but couldn't identify who was calling me. "Neil, come here." It was Jimmy, who was standing near the timer's bench facing the stands.

"What's up?" I asked.

"Check out the honey in the sun dress in the first row," which was elevated four or five feet above the ground.

"Not bad," I said, "but I've seen a lot better."

"You're looking in the wrong place. She doesn't have any underwear."

"Jimmy, she just winked at us, and caught us looking," whereupon she further opened her legs for better viewing.

Another timekeeper shouted, "Neil, the captains are waiting at centre field." Jimmy and I turned and bolted for centre field. I could feel Bill's eyes burning through my neck as we ran across the field. The captains had already shacken hands and they were waiting for us when we arrived. "What the heck were you guys doing?" Tom Clements, the Ottawa captain asked.

"Never mind, call it in the air," I said, trying to hide my embarrassment.

I knew that no matter what happened during the game we were in big trouble. How did the game go you ask? The game was a real nail biter and the crew was doing an excellent job of staying out of the players' ways.

But like every game, the outcome usually comes down to one or two plays, and our test came late in the game. Ottawa broke through to block a Hamilton punt, which went almost straight up in the air. It looked like ten NBA players trying to grab the ball off the offensive boards. One of the Ottawa players emerged with the ball and ran into the end zone for the winning touchdown.

Only one problem. We had a rule that prevented any offside player who was ahead of the ball from legally advancing it. Did the Ottawa player legally score a TD? I had absolutely no idea. Hell, I was happy to find out who recovered the ball.

As we headed for the dressing room, I knew the crew had done an outstanding job, but Bill would be all over us for delaying the start of the nationally televised game.

Back in the dressing room, Bill was at centre stage in command of the entire room as we waited for his game evaluation. Reading Bill's demeanor was never a problem, and he appeared unusually happy. "Neil, the man who recovered the blocked punt, was he onside?" he asked.

"Bill, I have no idea. Who could tell? All of the players were scrambling after the ball."

Bill hesitated, deliberately keeping us, particularly me, on the edge of our seats waiting for his analysis.

"TV showed that play several times and the man who recovered the ball was just onside, great call." He quickly moved on to tell the crew that we did a good job and the experiment was a success, and just as quickly he said goodbye, leaving us alone in the dressing room.

We couldn't believe it; not a word about the late start. I turned to the timing crew who were up in the booth with Bill and asked, "Didn't Bill say anything about the late start?" Luck was with us. Apparently Bill had to go to the john before the game and got back just after the kickoff.

We were leading a charmed life, but I knew Bill would find out because he didn't miss a thing. Sure enough, several weeks later he let me know what happened and to his credit it didn't go any further. I soon learned that performance on the field was his only concern, and that he was instrumental in giving me the chance to work as a referee as well as my first Grey Cup assignment.

The rule that an offside player couldn't advance a blocked kick made no sense, because all too often it was impossible to tell who was offside, and the rule was designed to bring back one of the most exciting plays in football, the return of a blocked kick.

The next morning I prepared a proposed rule change on return of a blocked kick for the following year because I knew if I waited I would forget. Sure enough, the rule was changed the next year and now anyone can legally return a blocked kick. Every once in awhile when I see a kick blocked on TV I can't help wonder what the girl in the front row is doing.

Officials, like players, are very competitive and when in a group will continually try to out-do each other, including trying to charm the socks off any unsuspecting female. I was no better, giving it my best shot but usually being totally ignored. After all, I was voted the ugliest guy in grade ten. Finally, one day in Regina I received the clear message that it was time to give up.

In 1982, our crew was assigned to do the Winnipeg at Saskatchewan Labour Day game. Thousands of Winnipeg fans made their way to Regina by air, bus, and car. It was just as difficult to find a hotel room as it was a ticket for the game.

The crew arrived on the same flight as the fans, probably the only flight into Regina on a Sunday. We grabbed a cab and headed for the Saskatchewan Hotel, a stately but well-worn railroad hotel. It was usually perfectly suited to a pre-game rest. The guests were either retired railroaders, purple blonds or seniors with wires behind their ears. There were no distractions.

But Labour Day weekends were different and when we reached the front desk to check in there was a group of more-than-attractive females from Winnipeg who were also checking in. The crew's antennae were immediately raised. It was the first time they had seen anyone in that hotel who could walk without assistance.

The crew was all over the girls like a bunch of bird dogs, and the girls enjoyed every minute. As a veteran, I was able to use my time-tested routine, which again met with the usual results: nothing. The girls focused their attention on the younger elements of the crew.

As we waited for the elevator, one of the girls kept looking at me. As we got on the elevator, she finally spoke. "Aren't you Neil Payne?" she asked sweetly.

Finally, I thought, my charm is working. And better, she recognizes me as the famous Neil Payne. Even the crew was impressed with my newfound attention, but unfortunately I couldn't resist asking the fatal question.

"How do you know who I am?" I fully expected her to speak of my great officiating career.

But instead, she said with that sweet smile: "Oh, I'm a friend of your daughter, Heather."

The crew, who had been watching the exchange closely, howled with laughter.

The elevator got smaller and smaller. Putting moves on your daughter's friend. Perhaps it was time to retire.

11

Has Anyone Seen my Black Hat?

By the end of the 1977 season, I had become the self-described best sideman in the league. I must be, I reasoned, since I had just worked two Grey Cups in a row.

Hap had just finished chapter seven of *The Peter Principle*, and had decided to move me to another position. My burning desire was to become a referee, but I knew it wasn't going to happen, even though the league had been desperately trying to find a new referee in the west to replace Paul Dojack, who had been retired for seven years. To make matters worse, Abe Kovnats, another veteran referee, had retired for the political ring. Hey, maybe I would get a shot.

Halfway through the season Hap called. "Neil, we'd like to move you to another position."

Finally, the black hat, I thought.

"Do you think you could handle working downfield?"

Shit, I thought. "Sure Hap whatever you want, I'll give it a shot." I hadn't worked downfield for over 10 years, but I knew if I were ever going to get a crack at being a referee, I'd have to work another position first.

After struggling for the first several games I began to catch on. Covering the receiver and defender was tough enough, but the real problem was getting into position so you could see what was happening between the two players. If you didn't, the players knew it and took advantage by pushing and holding on the inside, but I was getting better with every game.

It was not long before there was another phone call from Hap. "Neil, we'd like to try you in another position."

"Do you want me to referee?" I was now sure that my time had come.

"No, we'd like to work you as a line umpire."

"Line umpire? Hap, I've never worked as a line umpire, not even in amateur ball."

"I know, but we think you can do the job."

Again, I accepted the move. Hell, this might be as close as I ever get to the referee.

Maybe, I thought, it's not such a bad move. The umpire has the easiest job on the field. They are all so big, all they do is stand behind the defensive line and put the ball down after the play is over, or whatever the referee tells them. The only time they call a penalty is when the alarm on their watch goes off to remind them it's time to call holding. I should be able to handle that with no problem.

My first assignment was Hamilton at B.C., a good test because Hamilton's defensive line was as mean and ugly as ever.

Three plays into the game and my biggest fears were confirmed. Where in the hell do I stand without getting killed by these big apes? The pass receivers were getting awfully close to hitting me on their crossing patterns, so I decided to move up closer to the defensive line where I belonged.

The next play was a dive up the middle. I moved in quickly to mark the spot—too quickly and Larry Butler, Hamilton's left guard, stomped on my foot. I could tell from the throbbing from my big toe that his aim was perfect, and that I was going to lose my toenail.

For the next quarter all my dodge ball training as a kid paid off, as I danced from side to side avoiding the rush of the on-coming linemen and linebackers. In all the game films I had watched the umpire just stays there as the players bumped all around him. With all my dancing and prancing I was bringing a new dimension to the position, while I was just trying to stay alive.

To add to my problems the defensive line were now complaining on every play, "Watch the holding… No. 54 is grabbing my sweater… Can't you see him grab my face mask… No. 64 is holding on every fucking play, wake up and call something!" And on and on.

I told them I was watching the holding but was thinking, look you animals, I'm trying to stay alive out here, forget the holding, it's every man for himself.

B.C., who were having unusual success in running the ball, opened a huge hole in the middle directly in front of me, with Larry Key, the ball carrier, coming at me full blast. I had watched the umpire on a hundred occasions slowly turn like a matador and watch the ball carrier come within inches. I wasn't taking any chances and decided to bail out, quickly jumping off to the side.

Larry Key missed me by a mile but Ben Zambiasi, the Hamilton linebacker who was in hot pursuit, left his foot prints all over my back after he knocked me down, all in a futile attempt to get to the ball carrier. I had laid the perfect block. After the play was over, Zambiasi picked me up and offered me some valuable advice. "Ref, just stand there so I know where you are and I guarantee I won't hit you."

I had a better idea. Not only was I going to stand still, but I was moving back 10 yards where I wouldn't get hit by any goofy lineman. I discovered things weren't bad back there, even if it was too far away to actually see anything.

After several plays, the holiday was over. My buddy Jim Lysack was working as the back umpire and I had moved so far back that he was able to tap me on the shoulder. "Neil, are you the back umpire or the line umpire? Get your ass back up behind the line of scrimmage." I knew better than to argue and quickly resumed the textbook position, thankfully managing to escape any further major damage before the final whistle. Fortunately Hap was at the game and by half-time he decided that I wasn't really an umpire, something I could have told him before the game started.

Where do I go from here? My options were quickly evaporating. The league had decided to move me off the sideline and I had proved conclusively that I wasn't a line umpire, and apparently not a back umpire, although I had done a decent job in the short time I was downfield.

My assessment of my performance downfield turned out to be correct, but every official has his own particular physical characteristics that stamp his work. Unfortunately for me, while I'm deceptively fast, I run like a duck, and look like a duck, and the league concluded that anything that runs like a duck and looks like a duck obviously must be a duck.

Maybe the brass were concerned that I'd trip some receiver with my web feet, but I knew it was the less than professional appearance I portrayed trying to cover the wide ranges of the Canadian field. It was back to the sideline for the rest of the 1977 season. Had my chance come and gone? To make matters worse, Hap had appointed another

Winnipeger, Bud Ulrich, as a referee, and Bud drove another nail in the coffin by doing a great job. The chances of another referee being appointed out of Winnipeg seemed nonexistent.

After the 1977 season, Hap was forced to retire due to health reasons and Bill Fry replaced him as the director of officiating. Bill was one of the true characters of the officiating staff. He was equally adept at charming the pants off every stewardess between Montreal and Vancouver, or beating an irate coach into submission with his iron-fisted, no-nonsense approach to the quality of his officials, even when we were wrong.

Bill, like every official, found it difficult to leave the field when he became director. He wanted to take control of every situation, even things that happened on the field. We began to run pools trying to predict what Bill would do next.

It was evident from the start that Bill had different criteria in what he was looking for in an official. Being a former referee, he had an extraordinary talent in assessing what it took to become one. He must have, because before the 1978 season he called and told me I would be "one of his referees."

It was something I had worked toward for almost 20 years, had given up on, and now Bill was willing to take the risk on someone no one else was willing to touch: a decision for which I am eternally grateful. Just maybe, I thought, it takes a referee to know a referee.

Finally I was going to get off the sideline and away from all the coaches, the bitching, swearing, crying, moaning, whining, yelling, gesturing, criticizing, intimidation, and all around goodwill. Peace at last.

Other than fulfilling my one true character flaw—the absolute need to be in charge with the black hat—I wanted to be a referee to find out what referees and coaches talked about at their meeting at centre field before the game.

When we met at centre field I was instructed to obtain the numbers of the kickers, players who would be playing different positions, the quarterbacks, as well as the number of the designated import, from the team captains. It sounded like any other government job because in reality the Canadian game is all about imports and quotas. Once the facts had been recorded you were never certain what direction the meetings would take, but to say the very least they were all very interesting.

I remember when I was still on the sideline and Jackie Parker was made coach of the B.C. Lions, who were floundering and going nowhere. At the first meeting with the referee and umpire, Jackie had no idea what information he was supposed to supply or what to say, and he began to apologize. Kas Vidruk, the umpire, was prepared and interrupted Jackie and handed him a large box of aspirins. "Here, Jackie you'll need these," he said. "We'll look after the rest." So ended Parker's first meeting with the officials.

Most meetings were not so congenial. The tension for both officials and coaches is usually at its peak during these pre-game meetings, making it very difficult for either party to hide their true personalities. Don Matthews, whose ego will easily match that of any referee, usually brought a relaxed attitude to his meetings, knowing his team was well prepared and there was nothing further he could do. If there was a problem, it was intensely debated, but more often than not we were subjected to either listening about his mental jousting and psychological warfare with Ken Lazaruk, where surprisingly no winner had yet been declared, or listening to his crummy jokes, which were made worse by their interminable length. But no one had the heart to tell this coaching icon that he told lousy jokes.

In 1994, Coach Matthews brought his Baltimore Stallions to a late season game in Winnipeg against Cal Murphy's Bombers. As the visiting coach Don got to meet with us first, while Cal waited 15 yards away for his turn. Nothing infuriated a coach more than if he thought the opposition coaches meeting with the referee was lasting too long, and he was sure that the time was being used to tell that referee about all his illegal tactics.

Don was more relaxed than usual, and was trying out some new material, which was as bad as ever. While I was to listening to Don, I was watching Cal, whose patience was running out. He was pacing back and forth like a caged animal. You didn't have to read the papers to know Cal had lost the week before, and he could hardly wait to get at us.

Try as we could, we couldn't get away from Don and his stories. Finally after a couple of forced laughs, I said "Coach, that's it, we've got to go." But it was too late.

Cal was totally enraged. We had spent too much time with Matthews, learning about the Bombers dastardly deeds. There were times to talk to

Cal and there were times to listen, and this was definitely a time to listen. He started with last week's game. "That was the worse dog-gone officiated game I've ever seen in my life. We were screwed... Dave Yule's crew is the worst crew in the league." I might have taken some consolation knowing we weren't the worst crew, but I knew some coach in Calgary was telling Dave Yule that Neil Payne had the worse crew in the league.

The rest of the meeting was downhill. Our lousy officiating was killing everyone, from his team to the whole league. Don's crummy jokes had done the job. Cal was all over us for the rest of the afternoon and his cries of "Payne, you gutless wonder," seemed to carry an even increased sharpness. There's no doubt Cal's endorsement made me work just a little harder.

Coaching in the CFL is truly a fraternity, with coaches who are fired usually ending up on another team, fulfilling the prophecy of what goes around comes around.

George Brancatto, a life-long Ottawa Rough Rider player and coach, fittingly made his way to the other Rough Riders as a coach. George was a rather quiet, and sometimes nervous, man, with a subdued, but razor sharp sense of humor. Saskatchewan were desperate for a win and they were entertaining George's former Rough Rider team.

Other than the odd nervous chuckle, our pre-game meetings with Coach Brancato were usually very businesslike. But this time, the need for a win against his former team was written all over his face. As usual we asked questions that gave the coach the opportunity to complain about the other team's illegal tactics that he had noticed studying last week's films. George was quick to jump in, "Neil, I want you to watch No. 54 for holding, he's the best in the league. I should know because I taught him when I was in Ottawa."

One of our other pre-game duties was to check players' uniforms and casts to make sure they were legal. Vern Heath, who was my umpire, had checked the cast No. 54 was wearing. To make sure it was okay, and in an effort to reassure George that No. 54 would not be a problem, I was quick to point out, "Coach, we just checked No. 54 and he's wearing a cast. There's no way he'll be able to hold."

George didn't bat an eye or miss a beat and just as quickly suggested. "You'd better check that cast again. He's got a steel hook in it."

There was also an additional bonus in participating in the centre field meetings. I got a chance to meet all the celebrities at the ceremonial kickoffs. You can't imagine the excitement when I got a chance to meet Dick Assman, who Dave Letterman made famous, I believe because of his unique first name.

A lot of ceremonial kickoffs never quite worked according to the script. On one hot Sunday afternoon in Calgary during the 1980 season, I was directing the usual ceremonial kickoff with my usual take-charge attitude and choreographer's skill. Calgary was the best kept facility in the league, and the field, as usual, was meticulously clean and vibrant in the blazing sun.

I stood at centre field and blew my whistle for the ceremonial kickoff, when I smelled the unmistakable smell. I looked down and sure enough, I was standing in a fresh pile of horse poop that the Calgary mascot had neatly deposited.

Alone at centre field, I now waited for the ground crew to clean up the mess so we could start the game while the rest of the crew was having a good laugh. Not only were my shoes covered, but just like "Pig Pen" I managed to get some on my pure white socks. When I got back in front of the Calgary bench for the opening kickoff I asked them for a towel. There was no way. All I got was shots about how I smelled, and it was only after considerable begging and a half hearted threat to penalize Calgary for delay of game that a towel was forthcoming.

Regina is the home of the most faithful and hopeful fans in the league, and even Neil Payne received special attention. As part of every crew's ritual we walk the perimeter of the field when we arrive two hours before the game, still dressed in our Sunday best. Normally there is a handful of fans who are already in their seats. In Regina, every time I hit the 25-yard line I heard the same refrain, "Payne, you stink," which came from a fan sitting by himself near the top row, too far away to recognize, but I'm convinced it was one of my wife's relatives. At the very least, I thought, he could wait until the game started.

I believed I had all the tools to make it as a referee, and if I failed it wouldn't be because of lack of effort, or not knowing what had to be done. But I also knew that even though Bill was giving me the opportunity, I had to quickly prove I could take charge and gain the respect, not only of the teams, but of my own crew, an even larger task.

It didn't take long for that opportunity to arrive. Bill, like me, was a rookie, and whether by design or lack of experience scheduled our crew to work three out of B.C.'s first five games. Coaches tolerate officials when they win, despise them when they lose, and hold them solely responsible when they officiate in more than one of their team's losses. The season wasn't a month old and we had officiated in both B.C. losses, and two weeks later we were going back to B.C. for another chance with the visiting Bombers. Talk about going into the Lions' den.

In the 1970s and 1980s there was only one coach worse than Cal for going after the officials—Vic Rapp; yes, the Lions' coach. Not only was Vic as intense, ferocious, and emotional as Murphy, but he had a far more encompassing vocabulary to describe officials and their work, words that would have kept Cal in the confessional all day.

The beautiful B.C. evening hid what we knew was waiting for us when we entered the pass gate at the end of the stadium. The vendors were busy unloading their supplies as we walked down the long corridor under the stands. At the other end was a figure dressed in B.C. colours looking directly at us. He was too far away to recognize, but I knew it was Rapp. As we got closer, he started screaming and yelling about being stuck with us again, only in far more descriptive terms, disappearing before we got face-to-face. He had made his point.

I don't know whether Bill phoned ahead to say we were coming, or whether Vic was just waiting to confirm his worst fears. In either case, he was justifiably apoplectic. There was no way we should have been assigned to so many of his games, which is a problem in a league with so few teams. We weren't any happier than poor old Vic.

For added pressure, Bill had called to say the league was fed up with Crazy George, the B.C. mascot, delaying the game, and I was to penalize the Lions if he caused any delays. I had enough problems and I wasn't going to penalize B.C. for Crazy George unless I had absolutely no other choice. If the league were that unhappy, then let them fine the Lions.

I have mentally blocked out my pre-game meeting with Coach Rapp at centre field, but I seem to recall that at one point he pleaded like a condemned man that the league send another crew for the rest of his games. The players' not-you-guys-again look at the coin toss conveyed the same message.

Knowing a game has a potentially explosive situation has provided the catalyst for many crews to do some of their best work, and we were ready to show B.C. that we weren't their problem.

There was an uneasy silence at the B.C. bench as we lined up for the opening kickoff. "Neil, we've got a short delay," the coordinator whispered as we stood together on the sidelines.

"Now what?" I asked, even though I knew better than to ask.

"They're bringing Crazy George in by helicopter to land at centre field and they're a little late."

Just fucking great, I thought. If I don't penalize B.C., I get shit from Bill; if I do, this game is going down the tubes. What a choice.

Thankfully, the helicopter appeared overhead, looking to touch down near the sideline where we were standing. Beautiful; we were not going to lose too much time, and there's no reason for any stupid penalty; everyone should be happy. I moved closer to the chopper, which had landed, but George still hadn't made any move to get out of his seat.

In a split second, the draft from the chopper blades took my precious black hat and deposited it 20 yards downfield, with me in hot pursuit. I'd had enough, and out came the flag, "B.C. delay of game, ten yards on the opening kickoff." Coach Rapp didn't say a word. He just hung his head. He had seen this picture before.

I raised my arm to blow time in for the kickoff, but shit, there was no ball on the kicking tee. I quickly turned to the stick crew standing beside me, and they all had the same guilty look. Finally someone volunteered, "We forgot the ball in the dressing room."

In a split second, Coach Rapp was on the field and all over me. "You assholes are the reason for the delay of game, you no good... Why don't you go back to referee school?"

There was no place to hide, and I couldn't penalize him, because he was right. How in the hell do you play a game without a football?

But before Vic had the opportunity to really get warmed up, the ball boy returned from the dressing room with a game ball. We had the quickest kickoff in CFL history; even the officials downfield weren't ready, but Vic still managed to follow me the entire length of the B.C. bench, making sure I knew exactly what he thought.

The game was no better than the opening. The visiting Bombers and the Lions had a genuine dislike for each other and neither team was interested in playing football as the game quickly turned into a chippy affair.

To add to our problems, the Bombers had just traded Grady Cavness to the Lions. Grady was the consummate trash talker and if he didn't invent the phrase "mother fucker," he was there when it was discovered. Besides his mouth, Grady was capable of taking more than the odd penalty with his roughhouse tactics.

It was the type of game all officials hate, where law and order become the prime concern. I was finally getting my first big test, and I knew if I didn't take control, I'd receive a life sentence from Bill back on the sidelines

We tried talking to the players, but again it was like farting against thunder, a total waste of time. I'd seen officials try to take control by calling cheap penalties, a sure recipe for failure. Inevitably players lose respect if you start calling things you've been letting go, and once you've called one, you've got to call them all.

But time was running out. Grady was trying to intimidate his former teammates but the whole Bomber team was all over him and he was ready to explode.

Dieter Brock, the Winnipeg quarterback, rolled out to his right, one of the few times I'd ever seen him leave the pocket, and the B.C. defenders didn't want to miss the rare opportunity to take off his head as he headed for the sidelines, with Payne right on his heels. Just as Dieter went out of bounds he was hit late by the B.C. defender. Perfect. Out came the flag, and here comes Grady looking for trouble.

This time there was no trash talking. It was serious. Beautiful elbow Grady, I said to myself. You hit No. 62 right in the head. I'd already thrown my flag. By now Grady had lost it and punched another Winnipeg player in the mouth. Watch it, Grady, I thought, you'll break your hand doing that. A wild mêlée followed along the sideline, which moved into the B.C. bench, but miraculously there were no more punches thrown, as everyone seemed more concerned about getting Grady under control.

Some of our guys weren't sure Grady had connected with his haymaker. As far as I was concerned, he had caused enough trouble and it was a perfect opportunity to take control. I sent him to the dressing room after applying a couple of additional penalties. Several plays later someone else took a cheap shot, with the same result—more flags.

Suddenly all the bitching and complaining stopped. Both teams had at first declined our original invitation to play football, but now they knew we weren't going to stand for any nonsense. Even the B.C. bench was quiet; well almost quiet. Just maybe the "rookie ref" was getting some respect after all.

I had just taken the first major step in becoming a CFL referee and I had done it Bill's way. Bill Fry took a no-nonsense approach to how the game should be officiated. He could allow the odd judgment in error, but would not tolerate a referee who lost control of the game and turned it over to the inmates. On this particular night, we were able to keep the inmates locked in their cells.

The people who designed the size of the Canadian Football League field were obviously a group of referees. The extra width of the field allows a referee to stand at centre field and not hear the coaches screaming from the sideline.

I thought I'd found the perfect world. Other than the defensive linemen who complained bitterly about being held on every play, usually to the umpire, things remained very quiet. In fact the reverse was now true. Other than Wilkie, who like the defensive lineman bitched and complained on every play, no other quarterback would give me the time of day.

Even on penalty applications, Ron Lancaster would simply say, "We'll take the play," or "We'll take the penalty," and quickly turn away. Dieter Brock wouldn't say anything, but simply wait for the bench to tell him what to do, and I was sure Warren Moon had lost his tongue because he would simply point, and the rest were no better.

After Ron Lancaster retired I couldn't resist asking him. "Ron, why were you grumpy on the field? You never spoke or even smiled."

"Neil, Wilkie used to ask me the same thing. He used to tell me to loosen up and enjoy things. But I was so focused I couldn't think of anything but the next play. The 20 seconds to get the ball in play in the Canadian game is unique, and makes our game so fast-paced. There isn't time for anything else, particularly if you have to tell the wide receiver to keep quiet in the huddle because he thinks he's open on every play."

Come to think of it, as a referee I had the same problem; no time to think about anything but the next play, although I must admit I made a few friends on the field who liked to talk.

Bob Cameron, who was the oldest player in the world, became a rules expert on blocked kicks and challenged me every time a kick was blocked. Wally Buono thought I was his houseboy and wanted me to pick up his towel after he punted. Dave Ridgway always started talking before the game. Bernie Ruoff thought he was contacted on every punt, even when no one rushed the kicker. My favourite, Dave Cutler, liked talking during the game, particularly at time-outs.

It wasn't long before the light went on. All my buddies were kickers. Why? Because kickers were all considered flakes by their teammates, who wouldn't talk to them, so out of desperation they would speak to the referee, confirming that both species have a lot in common.

For my money, Dave Cutler was the best straight ahead place kicker ever to play in the league. His feats were even more amazing when you consider that his 5-foot, 7-inch frame was directly attributable to the fact that Dave had no legs, which up until then I thought were essential for a kicker. Maybe it was the Alberta winters, because Trevor Kennerd, another Alberta product who played for the Bombers, was the only other place kicker who was short enough to look Dave in the eye.

Dave was the first player who recognized that officials were actually human beings. After every Edmonton convert we'd jog together back to centre field. All Dave was interested in talking about were his cattle, or how I was doing. Hell, he was the first player who ever said more than two words without screaming or complaining.

But like every 5-foot, 7-inch player, Dave thought he was a barnyard rooster, and was always near the trouble, or causing it. One game, we had a fight near the goal line and he had come undetected down the sideline from his bench, and was chirping at the other team. I should have penalized him, but who else would I have to talk to? I told him to get his ass back on his bench, and I never saw him again.

Dave was also a practical joker and when combined with his relaxed attitude when he wasn't kicking the ball, contributed to his success. Kicking, after all, is the most pressure-packed position in the game, where in a split second you are either the hero or the goat.

Years later, I'm still the butt of one of Dave stories that he tells at the annual coaches' dinner in Edmonton. I've heard the story a dozen times and it doesn't change: "I had just taken the convert," Dave says, "when Neil yelled at one of our players to fuck off." Dave smiles at this point. I protest that it was the first and only time I ever swore on the field.

Dave continues. "I had never heard him swear before either, and I couldn't resist. 'Neil,' I said, 'your mike's on.' The look on his face was priceless. I thought he was going to shit himself. Finally be realized the mike was off and chased me back to centre field for the next kickoff, letting me know what he thought."

Well, Dave, you might have fun with your little story but I got even, big-time. Dave was getting closer to the league record for all-time scoring, and if possible, he was getting feistier than ever, no doubt wanting to get the record out of the way.

And Dave could be a real pain in the ass. Every field goal he attempted he thought was good. Inevitably he would turn to me after a long field goal went wide by several yards, and complain that it was good, even after it was waved wide by the guys under the post. Instead of telling him that he was blind, and that it was clearly wide (and besides, how can you tell from 50 yards away), I'd give him the politically correct answer. "Dave, the men under the posts have a much better view." But he was never happy with my answer.

As we got closer to the record, Dave became more miserable as he became more focused. One night he tried a long field goal against Calgary. The wind was billowing across the field and blew the ball wide at the last second. As usual, Dave turned and screamed, "Neil, that kick was good!" This time it was my turn.

"Dave, it sure looked good to me." I had pushed the right button. Dave took after the unsuspecting officials under the goal posts, who had a great view and correctly ruled the field goal wide. Who would have believed his little legs could move that fast. The downfield officials damn near had to penalize Dave to get him off the field, as he wouldn't stop pleading his case. "Even Payne thought it was good!" he told them, gesturing back at me as I stood near centre field.

After the game, the crew gave me hell for getting Dave all excited, but I'd like to tell you Dave, it was well worth it!

The referee has many roles, including that of a substitute parent, making sure the boys get dressed properly to play the game.

The league, in its wisdom, decided it was time to institute a dress code for the players, both for the players' protection and to portray some semblance of professionalism.

The players hated it because they claimed it took away their individuality, and it probably reminded them of when they were still little kids and their mothers used to make them wear their hats and mitts to school.

Well, who is going to enforce the dress code? How about the coaches? No way; the last thing a coach wants to do is discipline his players, particularly over a dress code. What about the league? No, that won't work because under the players' agreement we'd have to have a hearing and we didn't want that. How about the players' union? Infringe on the players rights? You've got to be kidding.

Who does that leave? You guessed it—the officials. Besides, they are the only ones who can't say no. The officials hate the job, because at best it disrupts the flow of the game, and at its worst heightens the already-elevated level of tension between players and officials.

There is nothing more difficult than telling a defensive lineman who has blood dripping from his nose and down his sweater because the man across from him is beating the crap out of him that if he doesn't tuck in his sweater, which is too short because the club tried to save a few bucks, that you will put him out of the game.

Your request usually draws one of several responses. "Go fuck yourself," which can be easily dealt with, or reluctant compliance with a look that suggested you had just taken away the last vestiges of the player's newly acquired manhood.

Initially we paid lip service to our new responsibilities, casually telling players to pull up their socks or tuck in their shirts, and generally taking no action if they did anything at all to correct the problem, no matter how half-hearted.

Bill Fry knew what was happening and pressured the crews to start making calls for dress code violations. I thought I would solve the problem for the officials by throwing Warren Moon, the league's high-profile quarterback, out of a game for three plays.

The league rule required a player's socks meet his pants. Warren's socks were so short that even if you put them on his grandmother's steel sock stretchers, they wouldn't be long enough.

I waited until the second half when, as usual, Edmonton had the game in hand and again told Moon to pull up his socks. He gave me the same sheepish smile as he tugged at his socks in a futile attempt to pull them up.

The next play, they were back in the usual spot. "Mr. Moon, you are out of here for three plays," I ordered, pointing to the bench.

"You've got to be kidding," he replied as he reluctantly jogged to the Edmonton sideline. I looked to the Edmonton bench, but Tom Wilkinson, the other Edmonton quarterback, wasn't moving.

I went over to the Edmonton bench where now everyone was

screaming, "You can't throw Warren out of the game," which was accompanied by the usual invective. The concern at the Edmonton bench quickly turned to Wilkie. "You've got to give us time to warm Wilkie up, you'll ruin his arm if he goes in cold," the coaches screamed.

Ruin his arm! Hell, you're up 22 points, I thought, tell him to hand off the ball and punt if you don't want him to throw. "You've got 10 seconds or I'm penalizing you for delay of game," I ordered, raising the ante.

Wilkie was quickly on the field, giving me shit all the way to the huddle. Perfect. Everyone was pissed off with the dress code; just maybe the league would get the message and change it from a penalty to a fine.

Does Wilkie hand off? No, he drops back in the pocket and throws a 40-yarder for a TD, and with it went my plan to get rid of the dress code for the officials.

Bill was still getting pressure from the general managers to clean up the dress code violations and, as usual, he was like a bulldog. It wasn't long before we were back in Edmonton for a game with the visiting Montreal Concordes, an awful football team led by high-priced NFL'er Vince Ferragamo and Billy "White Shoes" Johnson. Poor Vince. He threw a great pass, but I don't think he had any idea Canadian teams had 12 men on defense.

Bill had made one of his frequent trips west to take in the game and stayed dry and warm in the press box on a miserable wet night. The game was over before the end of the first half, with Edmonton having already put 30 points on the scoreboard. It was one of those games where everyone just wanted to go home. At the three-minute timeout just before the end of the first half, I got a message that Bill wanted to talk to me over the field phone. Shivering and soaking wet I picked up the phone and asked, "What's up, Bill?"

"Neil, Montreal are violating the dress code," he said.

"What's the problem?" I asked with no idea of what he was talking about.

"They've got the wrong undershirts on. They should be blue, not red."

"Bill, you've got to be kidding."

"Neil, I want you to tell Coach Eddy that they have to change their undershirts at halftime."

"Bill, are you sure?"

"Do it." End of discussion.

For the last three minutes of the half I couldn't think of anything else than having to tell Coach Eddy that his team had to change their undershirts. After the gun sounded, I intercepted him on the way to his dressing room and apologetically said, "Coach, you have to change your undershirts from red to blue. It's the league rules." I expected a less than enthusiastic response, but he never said a word. He just turned and headed for the dressing room.

There was no way Montreal were going to change those shirts. I could hardly wait to see Bill's next move, and I was sure it would end the officials' involvement with the dress code. What are you going to get me to do Bill, I wondered, tell Edmonton they can protest the game because Montreal have the wrong coloured shirts? That's pretty funny. How about calling the game? Or not letting any player on the field without the right coloured undershirts? Again not likely. I thought Bill had backed himself into a corner this time. I could hardly wait to get back on the field to see what was going to happen.

Our crew and the Edmonton team were waiting and ready to go for the second half, but still no Montreal. Finally, they came out. I couldn't believe it. They had all changed their shirts. I like to think they changed them because they were wet, but I think we were looking at a beaten team that had no fight left. It was also quite a victory for Bill. Even though he was in the booth, he was still able to control what happened on the field.

The dress code was there to stay, and in at least one case, it even affected the outcome of a game. The league had just expanded into the U.S. and our crew was assigned to do the opening game with Saskatchewan at Las Vegas. It was an exciting time, particularly for the two U.S. rookies we had on our crew, Bill Vinovich and Gary Cavaletto, who have since been plucked from the CFL by a major U.S. college conference and the NFL.

Ron Meyer, the Vegas coach, spotted the rookies and was all over them from the opening play. It worked because by the third play he convinced Cavaletto to throw Albert Brown, a Saskatchewan defensive back, out of the game because his pants were too short. Gary reported his penalty and I asked whether he had warned the player, to which I got a half-hearted affirmative response.

Albert was a known offender, but throwing him out on the third play of the opening game of the season was not my first choice. I had two options: ignore Gary's flag and send him back to the sideline to be ridiculed by Coach Meyer and perhaps lose him as a potential CFL official; or apply the penalty because Gary was technically correct. Hell, it was early in the game, and it's a good time to send a message. I put Albert out of the game for three plays.

Sure as hell, on the next play Tony Calvillo dropped back and threw a touchdown to Curtis Mayfield right over the spot vacated by Brown, which turned out to be the margin of the Las Vegas victory.

I spent the rest of the game getting messages from the Saskatchewan bench that Coach Jauch wanted to speak to me. You bet he did, but I never seem to get a chance to get over to their bench. By the second half, Alan Ford, the Saskatchewan GM, added his name to the list. I thought the latest episode would take the dress code out of the officials' hands, but no one else wanted to touch it, even with a 10-foot pole.

The 1978 season, my first as a referee, was over in a flash. I had worked eight years as a sideman before I got my first Cup. I wondered how long it would take to reach my ultimate goal as a referee.

I knew it wouldn't come early, because to get a Grey Cup appointment as a referee required the confidence of almost the entire league office, including the commissioner. But I was prepared to wait. As expected, I didn't get a playoff game that first year, but instead a surprise phone call after the Western final. "Neil, this is Bill. What are you doing next week?"

"Why next week? The season's over."

"How would you like to be the standby referee in the Grey Cup?"

It was Bill's way of saying thanks, and rewarding me for doing a good job. He had been on my back all year, but I realized it wasn't for things I had done wrong, but to make me better. I was gaining a greater respect for his obvious eye for talent. Three Grey Cups in a row; could things get any better?

The Grey Cup appointment was even sweeter because it came at a time when my officiating career appeared to be winding down, even though I still loved it.

During the day I would sit in my City of Winnipeg office in my starched white shirt, listening to the solitary sound of my mechanical calculator trying to calculate the latest subdivision, while snowflakes blew against the window.

Five hours later in Vancouver I would find the nearest phone booth and shed my Clark Kent clothes and change into my striped Superman uniform and take charge at centre field of Empire Stadium, looking up at the lights on Grouse Mountain while listening to 30,000 screaming fans.

The transformation was incredible. It was also a challenge. If you brought any of your Clark Kent thoughts or problems with you, you were dead by the end of the first quarter.

Officiating can be a brutal business and recent successes often signal oncoming disasters. It happened around this time to my good friend, Jim Lysack. He had developed some personal problems that not only could he not resolve, but that also ate away at his conscience.

The results were devastating and predictable. In a short period, Jim went from what I considered to be one of the truly best on-field officials to a man struggling with his performance, all as a result of his off-field problems.

It was my turn to help Jim, but we both knew it wasn't going to work. Many officials stay too long and have to be shot or dragged kicking from the field. Not Jim. He was a proud man, and he resigned. But with him went a large part of my motivation for continuing to officiate in the CFL.

It wasn't long before I made the same decision. Halfway through the 1983 preseason I received a rather large career promotion. My officiating career, which had been an asset during my 20 years at the city, suddenly became a liability.

I was starting to receive as much publicity as the politicians, and they suggested it might be time to evaluate whether I could officiate in the CFL as well as balance the high-profile position of director of real estate and land development for the city.

The message had been delivered. Although I wasn't forced to quit, I knew I would have a hell of a time trying to balance both careers and that in the end both would suffer. Reluctantly, after years of scratching and clawing and with a Grey Cup referee assignment in sight, I had to turn my back and walk away, just as the regular season started.

It was one of the smartest and most heartbreaking decisions I ever made. I was scheduled to work the opening game in Montreal the same day a story broke in Winnipeg papers accusing me and my new department of being the slum landlord of Winnipeg. As the new director of the department, if I had been in Montreal when the story broke I would have been looking for a new career.

My last game, while only an exhibition contest, was not without its memories. Edmonton was playing Calgary and toward the end of the game, players were taking liberties in a desperate effort to make the team. During a scuffle I caught two Calgary players punching an Edmonton player and decided to eject them. Usually it takes at least one player from each team to tango, but even after considerable discussion and prodding the rest of the crew couldn't come up with any Edmonton players who warranted disqualification. I knew the Calgary players had to go, and quickly sent them to their dressing room while I applied a 50-yard penalty, undoubtedly a Guinness world record.

Jack Gotta, the Calgary coach, was waiting for me at the sidelines. Whoever heard of throwing two players out of a game and applying a 50-yard penalty?

"Hey, Payne, what were they doing, punching each other?" Gotta shouted, loud enough that he could be heard in the press box. He wasn't alone in his commentary, and when one of his assistants joined in with, "Were the Edmonton player's hands tied behind their backs?" I couldn't help grinning, which only added more fuel to the fire.

I knew it was my last game and I savored every second and every play. I even enjoyed the screaming and yelling; it seemed like an appropriate farewell.

I thought was all over, but again thanks to Bill Fry it wasn't.

As soon as I told Bill I was quitting, he immediately asked me to stay on as a supervisor. I soon found out why. It meant spending weekends in Regina, and Bill couldn't find anyone else who would go. Not only did he have a brilliant eye for on field talent, he could obviously recognize management material as well.

After my first game as a supervisor I realized that although I was still involved with the officials, my new position was closer to my job at the city than being on the field with the rest of the crew.

I now knew how players felt when they were cut or retired. Once you leave the field, you are simply no longer part of the crew. It's still the same people, but the things that brought you together are no longer there. There is no sharing the feeling of accomplishment after doing a tough game together, or the pain of a missed call, only to rebound in the next game. Or the pure excitement of putting your ass on the line game after game. These are things that can only be shared and experienced by the men between the white lines.

12

U.S. Expansion—Ooops, It's Over

My years as an officiating supervisor from 1983 to 1994 coincided with the steady decline of the league, which I trust were totally unrelated events.

Attendance sagged, team owners, usually without deep pockets, continued to lose money before unloading or losing their teams. The league's credibility continued to slip as teams took turns exposing their financial instability, with the on-field product playing second fiddle to the league's financial and operational nightmares.

Don Barker and I would speculate whether the league would see each succeeding year. We both would have lost a lot of money, because contrary to our predictions, the league stumbled along year after year, seeming to have a life of its own, contrary to all the laws of physics and reasonable business practices.

But by 1992, the end was in sight and a major cash infusion was required. The first step was to hire a new commissioner. On February 27, 1992, at the football Hall of Fame in Hamilton, Don Barker and I anxiously awaited the introduction of our new boss and the last chance to save the league.

It was Larry Smith. He was young, good-looking, articulate, energetic, bilingual, a former player, and possessed both law and economics degrees and more important, he had a business background.

Listening to Larry captivate the gathering of media, owners, and league staff, I finally turned to Don and said, "This guy is too good to be true." He was everything the league was looking for.

Unfortunately, my comments rang true. Larry was just like the rest of us; no savior, only another human being with his own particular faults.

The expansion into the U.S. provided some much-needed quick capital, although probably not as much as anticipated or reported. Thankfully, the first team to join was Fred Anderson's Sacramento Gold Miners. Fred's love of the league matched that of any Canadian, and more importantly his financial commitment, including a $1 million dollar franchise fee, was instrumental in saving the league, at least in the short run.

Perhaps, understandably, Larry was too busy raising cash to worry about how the teams would operate, or whether the new American fields met the politically sensitive Canadian size requirements, leaving that problem to Don Barker and his supervisors.

Other than Fred Anderson's field in Sacramento, none of the fields met CFL standards. Only the Gliebermans in Shreveport, at significant costs, made the effort to ensure their facility conformed to CFL standards, while the rest of the U.S. owners were either unwilling or unable to do the same.

The Gliebermans, while often maligned, showed continued commitment to the league, even when it made little financial sense. The majority of the other owners were reluctant brides who knew little of their suitor and didn't want to risk losing their virginity or their cash.

Don Barker, who in 1994 was spending his last year as director of officiating, remembers visiting the stadium in Vegas months after Larry had announced Vegas as a new team. The stadium manager, was waiting for Don. "I wondered when someone from the league would come to take a look at the stadium," he said.

"You mean no one from the league has been here before to look at the field?" Don asked.

"Nope, you're the first one," he replied with a grin that reflected the problems that lay ahead.

Without measuring, Don realized that even pushing the sidelines out to almost the concrete stands the field still wouldn't come close to meeting Canadian standards. The field was widened but the sideline was so close to the wall that nets had to be installed to catch players that ran out of bounds. And it was still too narrow to meet league requirements.

There were, however, benefits for the officials on the widened field. In reviewing game tapes, I would rarely see the sideline because of its close proximity to the concrete wall. Art McAvoy, one of our veteran officials who when stretched out is no taller than 5 feet, 7 inches, was assigned to work a game on the sideline. It wasn't until nearly half-time that I realized he was on the game, when he inadvertently walked toward centre field. It was the first and only time he was in full view of the camera. It was probably the only game where an official had a perfect rating.

Baltimore was far more creative. Their end zones weren't deep enough, so instead of keeping the standard five yard distance between the markings in the end zone, they seized the opportunity to reduce them to four yards apart, until Don Barker recognized something just wasn't quite right when he did his pre-game inspection. Don finally measured the length of the end zone with the yardsticks and, as suspected, came up more than a few yards short.

The Canadian media took great pride and delight in exposing the under-sized American fields, as if their size would undermine the very fabric of the Canadian game itself. In practical terms, the minor differences in field size had no impact on the product, and in reality, field size was the least of the league's considerations when trying to sell new franchises in order to keep the creditors away from the door.

A larger problem for the officiating department was not knowing how many U.S. teams there would be for the 1994 season. A January 1st deadline to determine the number of teams came and went, and it wasn't until late February that the league announced that there would be teams in Baltimore, Shreveport, Sacramento, and Las Vegas.

It left us less than three months to find and train U.S. officials for the Canadian game. Finding competent people proved to be the most difficult task. Tier 1 and 2 U.S. college officials had already committed to their leagues for the upcoming year, and Don soon found that with existing CFL officiating fees, we were unable to attract experienced college officials.

Don, Ross and I met to finalize our recruiting plans. There was no time to set up a network of contacts in the U.S. and Don and Ross decided they would visit the U.S. and beat the bushes in hopes of finding some live bodies, and I would organize training sessions for the new recruits in a number of U.S. cities.

Don also identified a larger problem. We needed more referees from our Canadian staff, which was already short on experience. Ross and I had the solution. "Why don't we make a couple of our field judges, like

Ellis and McColman, referees. They should have no trouble doing the job," Ross suggested.

"That's fine," Don reflected "but then we'll have no one left at our field judge position, which is the most skilled position on the field, and we sure as hell we can't use any Americans in their first year."

Don was right. We would just create more problems. As usual, Don had a solution when we started our discussion, and used Ross and I to reject the alternatives, before springing his trap.

Looking directly at us, he dropped the bomb. "Ross, Neil, how would you like to help the league out and go back on the field?"

Ross and I looked at each other and started to laugh. I hadn't touched a whistle for over 12 years, and Ross, while only retired for three years, was 60 and in terrible shape.

Even before the laughing stopped my large ego kicked in. Why not, I thought, I know I can still do the job and I'm better than half the guys we've got.

"Look, I know it's too big a commitment to give me your answer now, but take some time and let me know," Don concluded.

The only meaningful thing I had valued as an official was my reputation, and when I retired in 1983, it wasn't as one of the best officials the league had ever seen, but I had done more than a competent and professional job, and had no trouble looking anyone in the eye. Why risk it all by coming back, I kept asking myself. I knew that if I stumbled, the critics would be out in full force, just like players who stay too long and are humiliated when they can no longer perform.

As often as I asked myself why go back, I knew it would inevitably happen, because of the need to prove that I could still referee at the pro level, and undoubtedly because of some form of mental inadequacy that suppressed all the logical reasoning for why I should stay retired. I also learned that my commitment to the league was far deeper than I realized, because when Don asked, I knew I would have a tough time saying no. I had worked with Don for over 20 years and there was no one in the league I respected more, or who had given more of himself for the league.

Before giving our answer, Ross and I decided to see if we were sufficiently committed to get in shape. Out of fear of what was ahead, I worked my butt off. I was at the local YMCA by seven o'clock every morning doing stops and starts on the basketball court before running the track and lifting weights, finally concluding with a ride on the stationary bike, which was more of a reward, because I got a chance to watch all the local girls in the aerobics class.

The afternoons weren't any better, covering 10 to 15 kilometers cross-country skiing at Birds Hill Park before heading home and collapsing. After two months, I realized that I had become the million dollar man and physical conditioning wasn't going to be a problem, but the burning question of why do it never left my mind.

With time running out Don and Ross headed off to the U.S. on their pilgrimage in search of new officials, while I set up training programs in Baltimore and Shreveport.

I called Ross in Baltimore to find out how they were doing, and soon realized they weren't. They would have had more success looking for Dr. Livingston than experienced officials who weren't already committed for the 1994 season. "How's it going?" I asked.

"Don and I have been interviewing for two days," Ross replied.

"Have you got anyone yet?" I asked.

After a deadly silence Ross replied, "We have two from Chicago, who said they'd lose weight before the season started." I knew we were in trouble.

Several days later, Ross phoned with the list of prospects, which included a generous sprinkling of black officials from the Baltimore area, and some self-professed red necks from the South. League budget limitations required that officials room together and I asked Ross to identify the red necks and blacks so I wouldn't put them together. He just laughed and said, "See if you can figure it out by their names."

A week later I stood in the classroom of the Baltimore Courtyard Marriott hotel, anxiously awaiting the arrival of the new recruits. The Chicago officials needed no introduction, as they had obviously misunderstood Ross' instructions, with one official trying to further enlarge his already rotund body.

We were ready to start, but we were still missing two Baltimore recruits. Twenty minutes later, out of breath, they burst into the classroom apologizing profusely that they couldn't find the hotel. Where did Ross find these guys, at the bus depot?

Halfway through the Saturday session it became evident that they all lacked the experience to make a jump to pro ball, and only the very lucky and mentally tough would survive, although to a man they were all dedicated and prepared to do what was necessary to succeed. The sessions were long and grueling and, as usual, I had brought in some beer for Saturday night. It was a great opportunity to sit and relax and learn more about each other.

We didn't break for dinner until about 8 p.m. and being a great humanitarian, I suggested they treat themselves to a beer before dinner. When I returned for dinner 20 minutes later, all the beer was gone. I knew it! It was those damn Chicago officials.

After the Saturday session broke up, I wandered down to the pool where they had all gathered. Dan, a Chicago official, was relaxing in the hot tub with a couple of beers. What perfect timing, I could finally see how big he really was. I plunked myself down in a chair directly in front of him and waited for him to get out of the hot tub.

Dan knew exactly what I was thinking and refused to budge even after we had exhausted every football and officiating story known to man while his discomfort became more and more evident.

I didn't have to touch the water to know the temperature was rising by the minute. Dan squirmed from side to side as his face turned a shade darker than crimson, as the sweat ran down his neck into the water, but he still didn't budge.

Suddenly, his breath quickened. Shit, maybe he's going to have a heart attack, I thought, and I quickly said good night and headed for my room, but turned to see him scamper out of the tub as the water level dropped by several feet.

All nine men who attended the Baltimore school worked their butts off to become CFL officials, including Dan, who lost more than 30 pounds in the next year. But only one made it: Boris Cheek.

It didn't take long to find out the problems our American brothers would expeience with the Canadian game. On the opening kick-off in the season opener in Winnipeg there was an American flag just as the receiver caught the ball. "Great," I though, "he's got the balls to make the calls."

What I didn't know was that it was a call for no yards, which is impossible on a kick-off. The referee told him to stick his flag in his pocket and get back on the sideline and behave himself, and things didn't get much better with our initial draftees.

Boris, like the rest of the young men, lacked experience, but his mental toughness, even temperament, and a patient Don Barker carried him through two CFL seasons, even though, as expected, his rating did not place him in the top group of officials.

Surprisingly, after two years, the NFL asked Boris to join their staff. Halfway through the season there was Boris on "Monday Night Football" making a call late in the game, which while technically correct, was unnecessary, particularly with the game out of reach. I couldn't resist. The next morning I called Boris, and without identifying myself started to give him hell about the call. At first he thought I was one of his NFL supervisors and tried to explain why he made the call. Then he realized who he was talking to.

"Neil, is that you?" I couldn't stop laughing and neither could Boris, still remembering. "I'm not in the CFL anymore and you're still giving me shit."

I asked him how things were going, fully expecting to hear how great the NFL was, but Boris was more interested in thanking us for the opportunity we had given him in Canada, and asking about all the guys. Not a typical American attitude I thought, before realizing it was a typical officials' attitude, where you never forget the people you went to war with, or those who helped you along the way.

After only one season in the NFL Boris offered, "If you can officiate in the CFL, you can officiate any football league in the world," something Don Barker and I had known for years.

The next stop was Shreveport, where Ross joined me, not only to help me with the school, but more importantly to keep me company. Shreveport reminded me of a suburb in Regina, only not as lively (except when the residents were killing each other). Finding things to do when we weren't working was a real challenge. And since we were still trying to get in shape we'd meet at 6 a.m. every morning in the hotel gym to work out.

As usual, Ross was the early bird, and was waiting outside for me to arrive. "Neil, it's raining," he said. We saw the water hit the sidewalk, but the sun was still shining. The humidity was so high the water was literally running off the metal eaves. Workouts were a breeze; all we had to do to work up a sweat was put the weights on the machine.

On Saturday night, desperate for some excitement, we decided to walk down the street and check out the action at the airport. In fact everything was just down the street. We couldn't believe it. Saturday night and even the airport was closed.

I knew Ross and I were getting close to being ready for our return to the field when for excitement we started testing our physical fitness by sprinting across the main highway just in front of oncoming cars. Not only did I know we were in shape, but we were starting to act like boys again, another telltale sign we were ready. Still, logic and reason kept telling me that after 12 years without blowing a whistle, it was time to give it up.

All that was left was to give Don our decision. I thought Gloria would be of some help, but as usual she left the decision to me. The rational side of my being had hoped she'd say I was crazy and tell me not to do it, but she never did, even though I know that's what she was thinking.

Finally fully committed, Ross and I said we were ready to go, and informed Don of our decision. Because of the pressure and stress of being a professional official and our ages, Don insisted on a full medical and stress test.

For me the stress test was essential, because at 57 I was the same age as my dad when he died of a massive heart attack while in perfect shape and health, and without warning. In addition, my younger brother Brian was snatched back from heaven's gates on several occasions after suffering severe blood clots.

The family chemistry wasn't good, but I wasn't worried. I had pushed and abused my body into the shape of my life, as I confidently walked down the halls of Seven Oaks Hospital to take a stress test.

Less than five minutes into the test the doctor yelled, "Stop the machine."

Shit, I thought, I'm not even getting warmed up yet.

He looked me in the eye and said, "We have a problem. I'm going to schedule you for an immediate angiogram. I want you to go home and don't do anything until we call you." I went totally numb; my world was falling apart.

A nurse helped me on with my jacket and wished me "good luck" in a tone of voice that said that's all that's going to save you.

When I arrived home, Gloria, like every good Winnipeg home manager, was out searching for bargains, and I was forced to keep myself company. I was soon convinced that only multiple bypass surgery and the heart transplant would save my life as I became increasingly disconsolate, lamenting life's missed opportunities.

But there was a bright side. I wouldn't have to go back on the field. The threat of death had finally put an end to the war between my ego and good sense.

But it wasn't over. Everyone knows someone who knows everyone. Thankfully, my contact was my next-door neighbour Verna, who knew every cardiologist in town. Two days later I was back on the treadmill, taking several other tests from outer space that Verna had arranged with one of the city's top cardiologists. The results weren't long in coming. I sat down fearing the worst.

"Neil, we've reviewed all the tests and can't find anything wrong," Dr. Hoeschen said. He suggested that perhaps the original tests had provided incorrect readings. "As far as were concerned, you can go back on the field, but the decision is up to you."

Great! Now what. My decision wasn't difficult. My family had a terrible history of heart disease, and I knew with my personality, stress was inevitable, and that it would take its toll. Why take the risk? I had done it all, and retired on top. Don was out-of-town for a couple of days, but I made of my mind to call and tell him I wasn't coming back.

I didn't have a chance. Once again my ego took control. What's the matter, afraid you can't do it? Are you a coward... How can you let Don down when he needs help... Life is full of challenges, have you given up? You'll question yourself the rest of your life if you don't go back... go on, show everyone you're not too old.

Two days later, I was on the phone. "Don, this is Neil."

"How did your tests go?" he asked.

"Great, I got a clean bill of health from my medical and I'm ready to go," I replied. There was no turning back.

The main school in Winnipeg in early May brought the American and Canadian officials together for the first time. How would the Canadians accept the Americans? Could Americans do the job?

Any question of how the American officials would be accepted was answered early. Boris Cheek was not only a fine young man from Baltimore, he was also black, and as an American he desperately tried to learn about the Canadian game. Ross assigned Boris to one of his first games in Shreveport, with six of his white brothers including a southern red neck or two for good measure.

Late Saturday night the group piled into a car, with Boris wedged tightly in the middle in the back seat looking straight ahead as the car hustled down a twisting southern back road. Dave Yule, a veteran Canadian referee and crew chief, secretly put a white bag over his head, and quickly turned to the unsuspecting Boris and asked him, "How do you like the CFL so far?" breaking up the entire car, including Boris. Whether you were black, white, red, Canadian or American, it didn't matter.

The veteran Canadian officials were true professionals and readily accepted the Americans, and more importantly, tried to help them make the grade. This was true for those Canadians who were on shaky ground, and might have viewed the U.S. officials as a threat to their jobs.

Most officials have the dream, if not the burning desire, to become a referee, and Canadian veterans anxiously awaited the announcement of who would be the new referees in the expanded league, many hoping to finally get their shot. Ross and I stood at the back of the room as Don prepared to make the long-anticipated announcement. As he began speaking, the room grew silent, many straining in hope of hearing their name. "Because of expansion it has been necessary to appoint two new referees, and both Neil and Ross have agreed to go back on the field," Don announced.

The group's reaction was identical to what Ross and I displayed when Don first came up with his brilliant idea. Everybody started laughing, convinced it was a joke.

The room again grew silent with the realization that Don was serious. Disappointment was written all over the faces of those who had expected to get the black hat, as Don quickly explained that anyone can referee, that's why he chose Ross and I, and that he couldn't lose the guys from downfield because they were truly the skilled positions, where all the tough decisions were made. Don was taking a hell of a gamble. If Ross and I failed, the GMs would roast his butt. But he was right, there wasn't much choice if you wanted to maintain any credibility downfield.

I could hardly wait to get started, and Don threw me in the spotlight right away: a vote of confidence or just poor scheduling? I drew the opening, nationally televised game of Saskatchewan at Las Vegas, complete with a first-class marketing job by the CBC promoting the game, using all the excitement of Las Vegas.

Don Aiken, our officiating supervisor in Vegas, met me at the airport and while I usually love the heat, the blast furnace I encountered when we opened the terminal doors was something I had never experienced. Don's late model car was littered with plastic bottles, and I couldn't resist asking what they were for.

"They're for water. In the middle of summer you don't go any-where in the desert without having them all full. In the desert, if you go outside and you don't have a drink of water every 20 minutes, you'll soon be dehydrated and won't be able to talk," he explained.

It sounded to me like a bit of American exaggeration, I thought, but I knew I'd get a chance to test his theory.

After our crew meeting, with our two American rookies in tow, we headed for the stadium, thinking about the heat as much as the game. The first thing I noticed when we got to the field was all that parking attendants had large water bottles strapped to their belts. Maybe Don was right.

I dropped my bag in the officials' dressing room and headed for the field for my first look. Ron Meyer, the Las Vegas head coach, and Mike Murray, a league V.P., were waiting for me. I could tell even before Mike opened his mouth there was a problem.

"Neil, only one 20-second clock is working," Mike apologetically announced. Before I had a chance to reply Meyer took over.

"In the NFL this is what we do..."

"Coach, I don't give a shit what you did in the NFL. We're going to do it the CFL way."

The battle was on, and there was no way he was going to push me around. What I didn't realize was the total frustration he was feeling, because there was simply no organization in place to look after all the needs of a professional football team. The 20-second clock was only a prelude to an organizational disaster unmatched anywhere in Canada, even by the government.

In the middle of my nose-to-nose discussion with Meyer, words stopped coming, although my lips kept moving. Don Aiken was right, I was dehydrating, which forced me into a neutral corner.

I joined the rest of the crew who were already getting dressed in our sparse but more than ample-sized dressing room. Even before my butterflies had a chance to fully develop there was a knock on the door. It was Mark Lee from CBC. "Neil, we don't have a dressing room. Can we put on our makeup in here?"

How could I say no? Even though it was the CBC, they were still Canadians. "Okay but please be quiet. We're trying to get ready for the game," I replied.

Before I could sit down, the Vegas cheerleaders walked through the door, claiming it was their dressing room. I wanted to throw them out but the crew kept yelling, "Let them stay." And I have to admit, they were leggy and gorgeous.

The only thing we were missing was the marching band. Another knock on the door; the marching band? No, it was the military honour guard complete with American-sized Canadian and U.S. flags. I hadn't been to the Shrine Circus for over twenty years but this was exactly how I remembered it.

Not surprisingly, the cheerleaders were able to find another spot, and we reclaimed most of our dressing room. I shouldn't complain about the Vegas dressing room because it was better than Sacramento, where we didn't have any dressing room at the stadium and used to dress at the university, then drive to the field on the tail gate of a Mexican worker's pickup truck, hoping like hell we didn't fall off. In Sacramento we had a tent located about 50 yards past the end zone, which by halftime was engulfed in darkness. Rich Rose, one of the new American officials from California, and his wife used to bring lawn chairs and barbecue hot dogs, which provided the only light in the tent. The only thing missing was the Beach Boys.

Ken Picot, my umpire, announced it was less than 10 minutes to game time and still no dressing room buzzer, a sound that I had missed for the last 12 years. "Come on guys, let's go, the buzzer isn't working," I said. We headed for the timer's bench to get ready for what we were sure would be an all-American pre-game introduction. The coordinator told us we had to go and stand on the other side of the field. In my 35 years of football we had never stood on the other side, but hell, this is Vegas and they were going to show us how it's done.

First the player introductions, with the cheerleaders all gathered outside the opened door of the Riders' dressing room, waiting to greet the players as they were introduced.

With music blaring, the announcer started his introductions. "Introducing the offensive line for the Saskatchewan Rough Riders, at left tackle, No. 62,…"

The music got louder and everyone cheered, but no one came out of the Saskatchewan dressing room. After what seemed an eternity the announcer tried again only with less enthusiasm, "Introducing at left tackle…" again with the same result, as the cheerleaders peered into the open doorway, but no one came.

Now greatly embarrassed, he announced, "I guess they're not ready, we'll get back to them later." Not ready, the players, just like the officials, weren't given any warning. The introductions were a debacle, but were soon forgotten.

We took our hats off for the anthem, for the first time on the opposite side of the field to where it was being sung. It was an embarrassing and disgraceful sight as the singer totally botched "Oh Canada." I contemplated sprinting across the field and grabbing the mike, but it would have been over before I got there. If the officials had been located in their usual spot, I guarantee we would have ended up with the microphone and finished the job.

I stood at centre field waiting to start the game embarrassed by what had happened.

In the end zone, the Posse were waiting for the signal to deliver the game ball to the referee at centre field. Finally the p. a. announcer asked, "Would the Posse please bring the game ball to centre field to referee Neil Payne." But they didn't move.

Finally, one of the cowboys on his faithful steed headed out of the end zone and right at me. He looked mean and tough but his voice gave him away "We don't have a ball; no one gave us one." I wasn't surprised.

When the game started, I was finally in charge; or so I thought. This was the moment Gary Cavaletto, one of the U.S. rookie officials, decided to put Saskatchewan defensive back Albert Brown out of the game for a dress code violation on the first series and Las Vegas scored a TD over Albert's vacated spot.

For the rest of the half, Al Ford, the Riders GM and Coach Ray Jauch, moved up and down the sidelines trying to get my attention, yelling at me every chance they got. In order not to play favourites, we called a load of holding penalties against the Vegas defensive line for tackling the Riders on all third down punts.

Jeff Reinbold, the Vegas special team coach, was screaming at us from the other sideline, claiming their holding techniques were legal. Coach Meyer, who made up his mind that he didn't like me in the pregame meeting, provided additional colour commentary.

I suddenly realized what I had been missing for the last 12 years, and I have to admit that I was enjoying every minute, even though I knew at half-time I would undoubtedly have a group of hostile coaches accompany me to the dressing room.

Sure enough, at half-time Coach Jauch and Jeff Reinbold were hot on my heels as I headed for the dressing room door at the end of the end zone. By the time we got to the goal line, Jauch seemed satisfied but not happy with my explanation.

Coach Reinbold, the fiery assistant, was prepared to follow me all the way into the dressing room, which thankfully was in sight, sharing his opinions on where we screwed up. Our door was locked and now I was Reinbold's prisoner. Then all of a sudden two 20-foot speakers attached to the end zone wall began blaring rock and roll music. Poor old Jeff, even though he was screaming, I couldn't hear a word he was saying, even though I could feel his tongue licking my ear. He finally left in disgust.

We spent halftime standing in the end zone being bombarded by those two gigantic speakers from which there was no escape. Of course, the air conditioning in our room was no longer working, and it was hotter in the dressing room than on the field.

Finally, it was over, and when Ken Picot reached to turn out the lights in our microwave oven dressing room, he noticed that the air conditioning had been turned off; probably the honour guard hit the switch with one of their flags when they were practicing sharp right turns. Just another routine day in the CFL.

After a half-dozen games it was time to evaluate how I was doing. Don Barker evaluated all my games and assured me that I was in the top group of referees, which didn't come as a surprise. I knew he wasn't giving me any breaks, because when I forgot to notify him that the crew was in town when we did a game in B.C., he lowered my game rating. Some friend.

In spite of the good rating, the only person I really wanted to satisfy was myself. I had originally worried about my physical conditioning and whether I could keep up to the players. I truly was in the best condition of my life, and it wasn't a problem even in the 115-degree field temperature in Vegas.

The toughest physical demands were the long flights from Winnipeg to the deep South. It wasn't unusual to leave Winnipeg in the afternoon and three planes later arrive in Shreveport at two in the morning, usually spending most of my time in the second-last row of the plane, next to the john with my knees under my chin, with some little kid hanging over the seat banging me on the head with his truck.

The biggest change in my performance was in judgment. I had spent the last 12 years reviewing hundreds of game films and officiating performances. Now I knew what the players were going to do even before they did. I knew exactly where to look, and what to look for. The most valuable lesson I had learned during my 12 years as a supervisor was what really mattered, and now, for the first time I was able to ignore incidental fouls that had no impact on the game, especially some of the clutching and grabbing between linemen that drives umpires and referees crazy trying to figure out what to call.

There was, however, one problem I had acquired while being locked up in the dark room watching film. I needed glasses, big-time.

Officials with glasses have always had a problem with credibility, and I was a glaring example. On TV I looked like Mr. Magoo looking through the bottom of two Coke bottles. The only thing missing was a white cane. My local optometrist said he could solve the problem for eight hundred dollars by providing special reflective lenses that were made for television. I choked, but told him to go ahead and order the pricey peepers.

In the interim I decided I would officiate without my glasses. I only really needed them to write on my penalty card, which most of time I missed because I was to busy doing something else, or making sure I knew whether the coin was heads or tales when I flipped it at centre field to start the game. Besides, it was only for a couple of games, and the last thing the league needed was a referee who saw everything.

To make sure there wouldn't be any problem with the coin toss I put a little nail polish on the heads side of the coin to make it easier to identify. Unlike the NFL, which is silly enough to trust the referee to be alone in these situations (which on one occasion resulted in a botched coin toss that cost Pittsburgh in a crucial overtime game), the CFL requires that the umpire follow the referee everywhere he goes just in case he needs help. It is a requirement that has saved many a referee, but I soon got tired of the umpire holding the bathroom door open for me.

I had one last game in Baltimore before I got my space-age glasses. Whenever I worked in a game in the U.S. between two American teams, I always made sure I had a U.S. coin, which I left in my bag, but on this occasion I couldn't find it. Great, I could just hear the screaming when

I flipped a looney. I didn't have any nail polish so I quickly marked the head with my black pencil.

As fate would have it, there was a ceremonial coin toss honoring the Special Olympians, who were represented by a young black athlete, who accompanied me to centre field with five gold medals around his neck. I gave him the coin to hold while I introduced the captains.

"No. 56, would you please call the coin in the air," I commanded as the young athlete flipped the coin high in the air.

"Heads," he responded.

I quickly looked at the coin and seeing no pencil marks announced, "Tails."

"No way, ref, that is tails."

I quickly got down on my hands and knees, fighting for a better view with the captains from both teams. He was right. Not only had my medal-clad friend rubbed the pencil marks off the coin, he had now gobbled up the coin and was heading for the sidelines.

I vowed never to go on the field again without glasses, which thankfully arrived for our next game in Shreveport.

After the game in Shreveport we returned to the hotel for a few pops. Making up for lost years, I hung on to the bitter end. Bernie Prusko, a 10-year veteran who had a very successful career (working four Grey Cups), told me he had had enough and this was his last year. We spent the night toasting the highs and lows of his career. Bernie knew it was time to go because he realized it was only the guys he was going to miss, and not the games.

We turned in at 4 a.m., leaving a wake-up call in hope of getting a few hours sleep before our 7 a.m. flight. It seemed like only minutes before the phone rang. I expected a wake-up call; instead it was Bill MacDonald, "Haven't you guys left yet? It's six-thirty."

In ten seconds Bernie was out of bed and getting dressed. There was no time to shower, or even brush our teeth. In Shreveport, if you missed your flight, you might get lucky and get out the next day. As we bolted out the door I grabbed an open bottle of Bacardi Breezer and tried to gargle away the terrible combination of too many beers and anchovy pizza.

Thankfully the plane was late, as we barreled into the airport waiting room.

I couldn't understand why the people sitting across from us kept looking at me. Had they never seen a thousand dollar Armani suit before? Now feeling self-conscious I looked down to see that I had put my socks on over my pants in a desperate effort to get dressed. Without batting an eye I told my admirers I was going to ride a bike home if we missed the plane.

I blurted out: "Shit, Bernie, I forgot my glasses back at the hotel." I quickly phoned the hotel and Bill assured me that he would drop them off when he went through Winnipeg. To make a long story short, the glasses made their way back to Canada, but I never saw them again. Eight hundred bucks down the drain.

The trip home provided only further embarrassment. I sat next to the typical little old lady who was old enough to be my grandmother. Just before arriving home, the flight crew distributed Customs declarations that had to be filled out.

The printing was so small there was no way I could read it without my glasses. "Ma'am, could you please do me a favour and read the questions and I'll fill in the answers?" I quietly asked. In a loud voice, and a speech pattern ideal for teaching kids in kindergarten she read the questions, which I promptly answered.

A businessman sitting in the seat in front of me now laughing, turned and asked, "What do you do for a living?"

I looked at him and said, "If you only knew."

"You must be an optometrist," he continued.

"No, for what I do, good eye sight isn't essential," putting an end to our conversation.

My first season back couldn't have gone any better. I escaped without any major problems, and finished in the top group of referees. I proved I could do the job. Yet in spite of my good performance, I was mentally exhausted and glad the season was over.

While physical conditioning was not a problem, the stress and pressure had taken its toll. Being away for 12 years, I founded it extremely difficult to concentrate and focus every second I was on the field, but luckily Ken Picot, my umpire, was there any time there was a sign of a problem.

I had promised Don Barker I would help out for two years, but he resigned as director of officiating after my first year. Ross took over as director and convinced me to carry out my promise for one more year. Wisely, Ross also convinced Don to stay on as a supervisor. Now I had two critics.

Life as a CFL Official

By the end of 1994, Don, the ultimate organizer, had established a network of contacts in the U.S., including Jim Keogh from Chicago, who started supplying the CFL with a steady stream of excellent recruits who had not yet reached the top level of college ball in the U.S. but showed tremendous potential. Even though expansion failed, the success of our recruiting and training was painfully evident when, by the end of the 1998 season, every U.S. official that we had trained had been hired by the NFL, WFL or one of the top college conferences.

Unfortunately, the expansion was not as well organized as the officiating, and when Ross and I visited Memphis in March 1995 to organize an officiating clinic, I realized the expansion was in major trouble.

We tried unsuccessfully to locate the Memphis Mad Dogs and finally phoned information for their local phone number. "Sorry sir, we have no listing for the Memphis Mad Dogs," the operator replied. After a few days of frantic searching, we finally found Adam Rita and his staff hidden in the back of a Fed Ex warehouse, trying to put a football team together.

The season was only two months away and the football team was the best-kept secret in town. It never had a chance.

After spending a year refereeing in the South, it was evident that Southerners lived and dreamed football, only it was U.S., four-down football.

Officiating in the South was an enjoyable as well as an educational, where football resembled a religious happening, with people literally prepared to risk their lives for the love of the game.

In my one and only game in Birmingham, I looked forward to a police escort from the hotel to the ballpark that Ken Lazaruk and his crew had experienced earlier. Sure enough, a police car and motorcycle arrived outside the hotel at 6 p.m. to escort our van to the park. There was no doubt that these large, fine Southern gentlemen were police officers, as Howard got out of the cruiser and introduced himself and his fellow officer, Delbert, who was riding the bike.

I pulled rank and asked Howard if I could ride with him in the police car. "No problem. Jump in."

Delbert led the way on his bike, blocking the intersection, which Howard then hustled through without any concern for the red light.

Delbert then leapfrogged to the next intersection to repeat the process.

Unfortunately the car coming from the adjacent side street didn't see either Delbert or Howard and just about hit us broadside. "Shit Howard, that was too close for comfort," Delbert's voice crackled over the police car radio.

Even Howard was sweating. "Not as bad as last year, he recounted. "I had to take one for poor ol' Delbert when Auburn was in town."

"What happened?" I asked.

"Delbert was stopped in the intersection and the car was heading right at him. I had to hit the gas and let the guy hit me broadside, so he couldn't get to Delbert. What a mess, but Delbert was OK."

Now it was me who was scared, and every time we hit an intersection my head was on a swivel. It wasn't long before Delbert was on the radio. "Mr. Payne, what do you think of our police escort?" he proudly asked.

I didn't dare tell him I was close to filling my pants and responded, "Hey, you guys do a great job."

It wasn't long before we were out of the city centre and Howard asked, "How would you like to operate the siren?" It was every kid's dream, and the only reason I wanted to ride shotgun with Howard. The dream was only 50 years late in coming but I gave it a try. Howard started laughing and said, "Look at them all run." We were passing through the projects and the siren had every kid on the move.

Once at the park the officers were never out of view and they were a welcome sight after the game, in which I was trampled and still had a headache and bruises all over my body, and anxious to get back to the hotel.

They escorted us out to the parking lot where I climbed back into the cruiser. The traffic was bumper to bumper coming out of the parking lot as well as on the main road back to Birmingham. Thankfully there would be no wild ride home. "Delbert, are you ready to go?" Howard asked, which was followed by the standard "ten-four good buddy" over our radio.

In an instant both Delbert and Howard, with sirens blaring, pulled out into the on-coming traffic, passing the long line of cars headed back to the city. It was dark but I could see the headlights of the oncoming cars darting to the left to get out of the way of our escort. It wasn't long before we were face-to-face with a car that had stopped directly in front of us that even the siren couldn't move.

Howard maneuvered the cruiser next to the driver's window and stuck his head out. There was a little old lady behind the wheel who was absolutely paralyzed without any idea of what was going on on that black Birmingham road. Poor Howard, he looked just like Rufus T. Justice from *Smokey and the Bandit* lecturing the elderly lady on proper etiquette when facing a police car that was on the wrong side of the road.

In minutes we were back in front of our hotel. I wanted to get out and kiss the ground, but I was distracted by a group of gorgeous flight attendants who were getting out of the cab in front of us. The next morning I called Ross and told him to forget about getting a police escort for protection before we all got killed.

While I continued to perform well in the second year, the stress and pressures were a constant aggravation, something every official has to live with, and I soon learned that all the things we had preached at our annual school of how officials react under pressure were actually true. Guest psychologists constantly told us that people, when under severe stress, will automatically react in accordance with the way they have been trained, even if a different reaction is required.

I was a textbook example. As a supervisor, I had introduced a number of new mechanics on positioning, hammering their implementation year after year at our annual school. Now, back on the field and under pressure, my mind blocked out my own new mechanics and positioning, and I automatically returned to the things I had done before I retired.

Ross was a stickler for mechanics and it drove him crazy if I was in the wrong spot. Field goals were a problem, as I continued to stand behind the kicker instead of beside him, as required by the new mechanics, where I could get a better look at the ball. He was the only one who noticed I was in the wrong spot and took great delight phoning me after every game to give me shit.

Finally, halfway through a game in Ottawa, I remembered that as usual, I was in the wrong spot behind the kicker. I knew the end zone camera was directly at my back and I turned and saluted the camera before moving to the correct position. The TV commentators were totally confused, as they desperately looked through the rulebook to find an interpretation for my new signal. Ross, who was watching the game at home, knew exactly what was happening and spilled his gin and tonic when he jumped out of his chair. It was a signal to Ross that I finally got it right, and there were no more phone calls complaining about my positioning.

Besides having a lot of fun (at least after the games), my officiating continued to improve, particularly my judgment, although I knew I wasn't still as mentally sharp as I was before I retired.

The size of my ego seemed to increase proportionately with my improving performance, and I began to think maybe I'd stick around for another year.

Experience should have told me that when things are going real well, trouble can't be far behind.

Our crew was working the annual Edmonton at Calgary Labour Day classic on a glorious Sunday Calgary afternoon. Calgary had the game in hand and more important, our crew was doing a great job. Edmonton took two penalties on a play near the goal line when Calgary had the ball. It required the application of two penalties, one with the restricted distance because we were close to the goal line. We misapplied the yardage and placed the ball several yards away from where it should have been.

After the game, I realized what I had done and self-doubt began. In my mind I tried to blame the guys for giving me the wrong information, Ken Picot for putting the ball in the wrong spot, someone for giving me the wrong spot where the ball was dead, and every other excuse except the sun being in my eyes. But even though it was only a couple yards, I knew I had blown it.

In all my years in the CFL, I had never misapplied a penalty, many of them far more difficult. While I never considered myself a great referee, I took great pride in considering myself as infallible when it came to the rules, and took great delight in matching anyone when it came to the rules and their application.

Was it only a momentary lapse, or had time taken its toll and was I beginning to lose it? Ross was probably the only other person who knew I had made an error. Ross, like me, was also a rules expert and for the last 25 years we had studied together, vigorously challenging each other on our rules knowledge, trying to beat each other on the annual exam.

Finally he had me, and he was quick to call me the next day to lower the boom, even though we were good friends. The fact that he fined me didn't bother me, but my mistake did.

I still didn't know if I had simply made a mistake, or I was no longer capable of wearing the black hat. I wasn't prepared to wait and find out and take a chance of embarrassing myself, or worse, put the teams at risk.

I had been in the league for 24 years, and when I walked off the field 12 years earlier my reputation and pride were both intact and I wasn't going to risk what I had accomplished. It was time to move over for the young guys and I told Ross there would be no officiating for Neil Payne after the 1995 season.

The rest of the season went off without a hitch with my final game in San Antonio with the visiting Tiger Cats. Just prior to the game, Mike Campbell, a Hamilton defensive lineman, sauntered over to where I was standing, thinking about the last time I would blow a whistle and said "Neil, I hear this is your last game. Too bad—I'm going to miss you."

I couldn't believe my ears and blurted back, "Mike, if I knew you felt that way, I would never have quit."

Other than yelling at me during the game, Mike had never spoken to me, and he was an official's worst nightmare. An absolute fearless and ferocious player, the rules were only a guideline for Mike. It wasn't a question of whether Mike would break the rules but only a matter of when, and we spent a disproportionate amount of time trying to catch him when he did. When trouble broke out, only one thing was certain; Mike Campbell was at the centre.

The game was over early with San Antonio crushing Hamilton 45 to 7. With the game out of reach, both teams were prepared to play out the string, but not good old Mike.

He was at his best, attacking every San Antonio offensive lineman with body shots, grabbing their face masks, pushing, hitting after the whistle, intimidation, and all his other specialties, some of which even occurred before the play was over.

Mike had the San Antonio offensive line right where he wanted them. They all wanted to kill him, and Mike wasn't backing down, while the rest of his team stood around watching their wacky teammate.

Matters were getting out of hand and a Campbell-instituted riot was a real possibility as every play ended with hand-to-hand combat between Mike and several San Antonio players, who were trying to take off his head.

In a last and desperate effort to bring the game under control I shouted, "Mr. Campbell, what are you trying to do, ruin my last game?"

"No way, I'm just trying to give you something to remember," he retorted. Thankfully, before someone got killed, Hamilton put Mike on the bench for a long rest. He was right. Mike Campbell is the only thing I can remember about my last game.

I sat in the dressing room taking my equipment off, again for the last time, fully satisfied with the job I had done in the last two years.

Even after a 12-year absence I proved, to not only to myself, but to some of my colleagues who thought I was crazy and would fall on my face, that I could still get it done.

I would stay on another year as supervisor, I decided, then call it quits. But I should have learned after three decades in the league that the CFL wouldn't allow me to call it quits. Ever.

13

One More Year

As enjoyable as working with Ross and Don made the 1998 season was, it was a perfect time to pack it in. With the Montreal franchise surprising everyone in the league by taking off under the leadership of Larry Smith, the CFL had some good news for once. Larry had sold the city on football again, one ticket at a time, and his miracle work in Montreal gave us all a sense that maybe, just maybe, the CFL was about to turn the corner.

But again, I didn't leave. I decided I would wait one more year because we had nominated Don Barker for the Hall of Fame. We knew he was a cinch to get elected. Don had officiated for over 20 years and worked 10 Grey Cups and he was one hell of an official. I wanted to be there when he was finally inducted.

It was something both Ross and I didn't want to miss; we couldn't afford to, because they only elect an official into the hall every 20 years. The last one had been Paul Dojack in 1978.

As planned, Don was elected into the hall with the official ceremony scheduled to take place in October 1998, and Ross and I made plans to join him in Hamilton for the celebrations.

So finally, it was a perfect time to say goodbye to the league and the guys that I had gone to war with for the last 30 years.

But then, at our annual school in May, Ross started to feel lousy and sure enough he was diagnosed with the dreaded cancer. But hey, no problem he was going to have early treatment and we'd still get together in Hamilton to join Don for the big celebrations.

As the induction date approached Ross finally said he felt too lousy and had to pass, which took an edge off the festivities.

Two weeks later, on October 29, with a game in Winnipeg that night, I woke up to an early morning phone call with that unmistakable long distance ring. What does Ross want this early in the morning, I thought as I picked up the phone? But it wasn't Ross; it was his wife, Joan. "Neil, Ross is gone, he just passed away."

I couldn't find any words. How could he have died? They hadn't even started his treatment.

With all due respect to the true soldiers and armies of this world, I now have some appreciation and understanding of how they feel when their comrades fall in action. Suddenly our 30 years together were vividly replayed in my mind with all of the clarity and sharpness of an instant replay, only it was weighted with the emotions we had shared both on and off the field. I remembered all those times I desperately needed help, and I knew Ross would be there when others would have turned their backs. Or after having a shitty game, the phone would ring, and by the time he hung up I knew the sun would shine the next morning. And yes, the many great times that were made all the more enjoyable by the tough times we'd battled our way through.

The crew was already on its way to Winnipeg, unaware of Ross's death. I waited for them to arrive in the hotel lobby, something Ross and I had done together for the past 15 years at the annual school. Now, alone, I greeted the crew as they walked through the front door. It was a very difficult and emotional experience because it was a senior crew. Dave Hutton, Bill Harcourt, Jacques Decarie and Don Ellis had not only worked with Ross on the field but, like me, had known him for years as a friend.

The rest of the day our thoughts were anywhere but on the football game. But the crew had no choice; they had to work the game. Football officiating requires a hundred percent concentration, and I was concerned that we might have a disaster on our hands that night. I should have known better. The crew did a hell of a job, and they didn't do it for themselves. The post game meeting lasted longer than usual, with a proportional increase in beer consumption. The meeting was finally called because of sunlight. But we had not come close to exhausting our "Rossi" tales. We would have to save them for another day.

Ed Chalupka asked me to take charge of the officiating for the rest of the year. The only significant difference was that I now had to look after all of the complaining coaches instead of just a few, which was almost a full-time job.

At the end of the season I was totally exhausted but completely satisfied, particularly with the Grey Cup. As Gloria and I made our way back to the hotel, I asked her to remind me to tell the league that I'd had enough if they asked me to take the director's job on a permanent basis. But I had this gnawing feeling that I wouldn't say no because of all the work Don, Ross and I had put in trying to develop officials for the league, particularly during the wacky U.S. expansion. I told myself that I didn't want to leave until they had someone qualified in place.

But thankfully there was a good chance I wouldn't get a chance to say yes or no, because when offered in the past I flatly refused to move to Toronto, which was a requirement for the job.

After the season, it wasn't long before Ed Chalupka, the league vice-president, made the offer. He asked me to become the permanent director of officiating. My response, that I wouldn't move to Toronto, didn't have the desired effect. Ed simply said, "Okay, you can do it from Winnipeg."

After 30 years with the struggling league I couldn't deny my total commitment to and love for this Canadian institution, even if it was the subject of ridicule and criticism for its problems, real and imagined. Even I had to admit that no professional sports league faced more challenges than the Canadian Football League if it were going to survive over the long-term.

I looked at Ed and thought: how can I say no? Ross was gone and Don had retired. We both knew that I was the last man standing.

Afterword

The Greats

One of the great privileges of spending a lifetime officiating in the CFL is the up-close view you have of some of the finest athletes in the world. And writing about my years in the league wouldn't be complete without a few words about the first among equals: the CFL quarterbacks.

Who was the best quarterback to play in the CFL? Comparing players from different eras can be a futile exercise, because there is no direct comparison, although in the case of quarterbacks there are always statistics, which again don't always show the real winners. However one thing is certain; today's players are quicker, bigger, faster, and stronger than they were 25 years ago.

While reluctant to make comparisons of players from different eras, I have had the unique opportunity to stand face to face with these leaders and look into their eyes when the game was on the line, and watch the results, which many times were predictable.

Quarterback watching was something I did over a period of 25 years, although from my referee's position I must admit that I was as familiar with their rear ends as I was with their faces. You'd think after all those years I'd know something about who is the best, that is if I knew anything about the game other than throwing flags.

How tough is it to be a quarterback in the CFL? The 20-second rule to put the ball in play and only three downs put incredible pressure and responsibility for success directly on the quarterback. Instinctively the quarterback must know what play to call next, because he doesn't have time to second-guess himself, and with only two downs to gain a first down there is virtually no room for poor execution.

How good are CFL quarterbacks? If you take the names Theismann, Moon, and Flutie, they were equally as prominent playing for NFL teams after playing in the CFL. The reverse was not always true. Vince

Ferragamo, the Los Angeles Rams celebrity and Billy Joe Tolliver, a real gentleman on the field when he played for Shreveport, and now back in the NFL, were less than successful in the CFL.

To me, the quarterbacks who were the real winners were those who in spite of their own physical limitations, or when faced with almost certain defeat, found a way to win.

Ron Lancaster of the Saskatchewan Riders and Edmonton's Tom Wilkinson possessed more than their share of these qualities. These two men were similar in many respects, both putting the ultimate stamp on their careers with Grey Cup victories, with Tom managing four Grey Cup victories during the Edmonton dynasty of the late 1970s and early 1980s.

Both men were produced from the same football cookie cutter. They were both short and dumpy. Physically gifted they weren't. Their physical limitations were more than overshadowed by their desire and competitiveness and the need to win (although as a referee I could have done without Wilkie's bitching and complaining on every play).

Lancaster had the uncanny ability to find the other team's weakness and exploit it play after play, even if it meant running George Reed six or seven plays in a row. George could barely pick himself off up the ground and before he got back to the huddle, Ron had called his number again. George never complained. In fact, George never complained about anything. The two things officials hate most is a ball carrier complaining about the way they've been hit, and defensive linemen screaming they are being held. George was hit more often than any other ball carrier, and often they were late hits, but he never complained, although half the time I think it was because he was too damn tired.

Lancaster was a pocket passer, which made it doubly difficult for a guy who looked like an overgrown jockey. Fans watching on TV can't understand why a quarterback can't find an open receiver. For Ron, it was doubly difficult, and sometimes impossible, because there was no way he could look over top of the lineman and was forced to find an alley between them. The referee and quarterback both look in the same direction, the quarterback looking for a receiver, the referee at the defensive lineman coming to kill a quarterback or block the pass.

All too often it appeared that there was nowhere to throw the ball and Ronnie was going to get sacked, when suddenly a small opening would occur between the tackle and guard and Ron would release the ball just before being hit. Contrary to good officiating mechanics, I would look downfield following the flight of the ball with no receiver in sight and think, where in the hell is he throwing it? Suddenly the Rider receiver would cut across the middle and make the catch. There was no one better at finding an open spot where none existed.

Like Wilkie, it was Ron's competitiveness that made him a winner and there were many nights when he was bruised and battered and left the field adjusting his shoulder pads muttering to himself because he was hit so often: and even though he got pissed off, his eyes never quit. He honestly believed he could always win and often did if there were enough time left on the clock.

I have sat with Ron on the rules committee and there have been the number of proposals to cut down the length of the last three minutes, which all too often in a dull game can seem like an eternity. As a coach, he continually opposes any change because the competitiveness still remains, and he still believes if he can get the ball back one more time, he can still win.

Wilkie's competitiveness left no doubt as to who was the leader of the Eskimos. Like Lancaster, he used every weapon at his disposal, which were numerous; and whether you were a player or an official, he always kept you on your toes. It wasn't until the game was on the line that we saw the true Wilkie, combative, cranky, with the desperate need to win. I'm sure he would have used his own mother as a bargaining chip if it meant victory.

Tom liked to use all his weapons but when the passing game wasn't working and the backs weren't getting any yards on the ground, which wasn't often, he put the responsibility of winning on his own shoulders, and usually pulled it off. You could smell it coming; Edmonton couldn't move the ball, the score was tight and the opposition started to believe they could win, but Wilkie had two cards. With the opposition defense gaining confidence and now coming real hard, Wilkie, at the appropriate moment, would draw them offside for a crucial first down, and with it went the momentum of the game.

If drawing the opposition offside didn't work, he had one last card; he would run. Tom used to run like Leo Lewis, the great Bomber back in the '50s, with his hips gyrating. Only when Tom did it, he looked like he was waddling. But he always got the first down, and I don't mean one or two yards. If he needed seven, he got eight, if he needed 10, he got 11.

Who were the strongest passers? Notice I didn't say the best, although I think that both Dieter Brock, a Winnipeg quarterback, and Warren Moon were the best deep throwers.

Moon and Brock were completely different than Lancaster and Wilkinson. Both were physically gifted, as well as the strong silent types. The leadership they provided was as a direct result of their play on the field. Poor Dieter; the only time he opened his mouth was to say that there was nothing to do in Winnipeg except to visit the Winnipeg Zoo, which alienated all too sensitive Winnipegers.

Brock was physically the strongest quarterback I have ever seen. Not only did he have a true rifle for an arm, but the rest of his body was equally as strong. It had to be. Winnipeg's offensive line gave the opposition countless opportunities to hit Dieter, who was also his worst enemy by holding onto the ball until the last second. He was the only quarterback I knew who could throw the ball 60 yards downfield off his back foot while being hit, all with amazing accuracy.

Teams kept hitting him high with the same apparent effect; they either bounced off or, rarely, knocked him to the ground. Either by design or chance, teams started hitting him in the knees, finally injuring one. I thought it might mercifully end his career but then on went the brace, and it was business as usual. He got hit as often and as hard as any quarterback, sometimes inviting the contact, but just like George Reed, he never complained.

Warren Moon is probably the best pure passer ever to play in the CFL, even though the brute power of the Edmonton dynasty infrequently required him to push his skills to the limit. Even in his CFL days, Warren was the prototype NFL quarterback.

His passes were picture perfect, tight spirals that looked like missiles always reaching their target. It didn't matter whether it was 25 or 50 yards, Warren was always accurate. He was the only quarterback I can remember consistently and accurately throwing tight spirals into western hurricane winds.

How about the toughest quarterback in the league? Without a doubt Matt Dunigan. That was Matt's big problem; he was too tough.

By its very rules, CFL quarterbacks take far more punishment than their NFL brothers who are protected by an in-the-grasp rule and absolutely no contact above the shoulders. In addition, CFL referees appear to be more lenient in permitting hits to the quarterback. When comparing quarterback injuries between the leagues, the durability of the Canadian quarterback is amazing.

But Matt had one problem. Not only did he invite contact, but all too often he initiated it. Matt spent too much time in Edmonton watching the great Edmonton linebacker, Dan Kepley, and he thought that just like Dan he could challenge people and run through them or knock them down.

When he arrived in Winnipeg in 1992 his body was already racked with numerous injuries from his shoulders to his toes, and it was time for the veteran quarterback to start acting his age.

Not likely. He worked himself into a miniature Hercules in the off-season and took on all comers. Matt finally hit the mother lode and signed with Birmingham in 1995. He almost got me killed when Saskatchewan visited Birmingham. Matt was intercepted and long after the play was over, decided to knock the crap out of the player who intercepted his pass. My flag was out in a second and I stepped in front of Dunigan to prevent further problems from the Saskatchewan players who were trying to get at him.

Good old Matt decided to take on the entire Saskatchewan team. In a split second I was on the ground with 24 players trampling all over me. The game film showed I was stomped on and kicked more than 20 times in the head, hands, legs, stomach and of course in the rear end. Every time I got close to getting up someone else knocked me down.

When it was finally over I had five new holes in my body, with blood pumping out like a Texas oil well.

It was during the height of the AIDS scare, and while both trainers came on the field, no one would come near me, never mind touch me. Finally the Birmingham trainer, behind a wall of plastic, patched me up.

I had trouble remembering where I was, but I had no trouble remembering to throw Dunigan out of the game. Ross Perrier, the new director of officiating and a good friend, offered to finish the game, but I knew I'd never live it down if I let him complete the job. I told him to take a hike.

When Matt broke into the league in 1983, I thought he was a great player but only an average quarterback. He was the only player I knew who got better at his position every game until he was dragged from the field for the last time.

In 1995 in Winnipeg he put on the single most impressive display of passing ever witnessed in the CFL and I suspect in any other league. Matt threw for 700 yards, a record in any Guinness book, never missing a receiver with three or four passes traveling 60 yards before literally falling into the receivers hands over their shoulder while they were running at full speed.

Incredibly, Matt again kept coming back from all his injuries to legs and shoulders and even an Achilles tendon late in his career. Unable to destroy his body, Matt took several bad hits to the head and brain, which could not be repaired with burning desire and rehabilitation. Mercifully, he was forced to retire as not only the league's toughest quarterback, but also one of its most colourful and skilled.

Who was the best quarterback in the CFL? First of all, what does it take? Quickness, some speed, a good arm, and just as important, physical and mental toughness to get the job done no matter what the circumstances: and like the great players in any sport, the intuition of what to do next.

Tom Clements, a Notre Dame graduate, while not being overly talented physically, possessed all the necessary qualities, and more importantly used them in a very successful CFL career, winning Grey Cups in both the east and west for Ottawa and Winnipeg.

But who is the best? Without a doubt it's Doug Flutie, whose greatness goes well beyond the records and awards he has established. While there were other quarterbacks with Doug's speed, his quickness and ability to avoid contact from would-be tacklers is unmatched.

When I refereed my first game with Doug in 1994, it reminded me of the touch football game that we used to play in the park, where we had no offensive line and the defense was supposed to count to two before rushing the quarterback, but never did. Doug was so quick in getting rid of the ball that even unblocked the defensive line couldn't get to him. I'm sure the only reason Calgary had an offensive line was because the rules require that you must have five lineman on the line of scrimmage at the snap. Refereeing his games was a dream, because no one ever came close to hitting him. But you had to be in great shape.

Early in the game he would run right, then left, then right again before throwing downfield, repeating the same recipe several times before the end of the first quarter. Not only was the defensive line like whipped dogs, so was I. Finally I told him, "Mr. Flutie, stop running around. You're killing me." He didn't bat an eye, because he was too busy thinking about the next play.

What about his arm, which is often questioned by his critics along with everything else? Make no mistake—Doug can throw the ball. Not only does his record show it, but even under tight coverage in the NFL he can put it where he wants. If he has a fault, it is sometimes throwing the ball when he shouldn't, while believing if he doesn't get the job done, he'll get you on the next series.

Physical and mental courage can often be the difference between winning and losing, and even here Doug had lots of critics. In the 1993 Western final, the heaters broke down his hands were frozen to the point where he could no longer grip the ball. Even as a crummy official I've known that feeling and once your fingers are frozen, throwing becomes impossible. But Doug still had to shoulder the responsibility for the loss.

Doug Flutie was also a marked man, with every team trying to take his head off, some illegally. In Las Vegas there was very little room between the sideline and stands, and the team installed a net to catch players before they hit the concrete wall. On a quarterback sweep Doug ran out of bounds, and I was in hot pursuit to make sure there was no nonsense after the play finished, particularly with the concrete wall staring the players in the face as soon as they hit the sideline.

Sure enough, long after Doug had stepped out of bounds a Las Vegas linebacker tried to make a name for himself by putting Doug through the wall. As with all great athletes, Doug had a sixth sense and ducked at the last second. The Vegas player's head is still stuck in that concrete wall. Flutie looked at me, but never said a word as he went back to the huddle. It was a challenge he faced game after game, but rarely did anyone ever catch him with a solid hit, although everyone tried.

Doug has very slender features and looks like the farthest thing from a football player. During the 1996 Grey Cup I stood at field level with both teams waiting for pre-game introductions. The adrenaline, emotion, and focus of the players is impossible to describe, but it sent shivers up and down my back. Massive men getting ready to do battle, with oversized muscles twitching from tension, totally focused on physically destroying their opponent.

In the middle of the Toronto team was a small man, with slender features who looked like he should have been the water boy, but wasn't, because he was wearing a uniform. It was Doug! He looked like a boy whose parents had sent him to a violin lesson, taken a wrong turn, ended up in the players' dressing room and was forced to put on a uniform. He just didn't fit in. He was too small and slender, and his withdrawn demeanour was totally out of place amongst his totally psyched teammates, who now more closely resembled caged beasts than normal men.

Doug's physical courage never failed, continually running wide and up the middle throughout his whole career, facing the reality of a linebacker or defensive back trying to bury him every time he did. While Doug possessed all the physical tools, it was his mental courage, the will to win and unfailing intuition that makes him truly great.

It's easy to win when you're ahead, but to win when everyone else says you can't is the mark of greatness.

Throughout his whole career, Doug has had the burden of being told he's not good enough, not only by the so-called experts in his own country, but also by some north of the border. How many of us would be able to perform our jobs if our bosses continually told us we weren't good enough?

If the criticism affected Doug, it was only to make him better. There were games when nothing went right but his attitude was, give me one more chance and we'll win, a thought shared by every man in that huddle.

What makes the last three minutes of the Canadian game so exciting is that it gives the great players one more chance to win, which they often did. Doug's play calling and execution in these situations was incredible, rarely making a mistake in judgment or execution, often finding receivers in the last second after the play had broken down.

Flutie matched Wilkie's desire and need to win, and like Wilkie, when the game was on the line he would take matters into his own hands, only with considerably more physical skill. The defense knew that even on a second and long with the game on the line, Doug was likely to run the quarterback draw, which they seemed helpless to stop.

Many times he was touched, grabbed or cornered but just like Wilkie, he always managed to get the first down, and if he didn't do it with the run, he'd complete a last-minute desperation pass, which set up the ultimate victory.

Doug must have watched some of Wilkie's films, because while

Wilkie invented drawing the defense offside while he was over the centre, Flutie perfected it from the shotgun position, and when the time was right he didn't hesitate to use it. The defensive line, which was now desperate to put some pressure on Doug, inevitably tried to get a quick jump at the snap, and was easy pickings for Doug's new tactics.

He would thrust his hands and right foot forward and scream for the ball, but the only thing that came was the defense and a five yard penalty, always at a crucial time.

Doug's physical talents and records make him the greatest quarterback in CFL history. His ability to win when given one more chance puts him a class by himself.

I have no business discussing quarterbacks whose rear ends I can't recognize, but Jackie Parker, the Edmonton great of the '50s and '60s, must be included in any list. Jackie was simply a great football player who played quarterback, among other positions. Jackie, like Doug, had the ability to win when given just one more chance, many times with what appeared to be impossible circumstances, whether on offense or defense.

In the dying seconds of the 1954 Grey Cup, Jackie ended up returning a fumble the entire length of the field, upsetting the Montreal Alouettes and establishing a long-lasting Edmonton dynasty.

There isn't a CFL fan in the west who doesn't have nightmares about Jackie Parker beating their hometown team when it appeared to be headed for the Cup.

You can't, without fear of bodily harm, talk about quarterbacks without mentioning the linemen who were either trying to protect them or take the quarterback's head off, depending what side of the line of scrimmage they were on.

Being a referee was a perfect job, except for having to listen to the defensive linemen. They reminded me of whiny kids who you can still hear, even if you send them to their rooms. They bitch and complain before, during and after every play. "Hey ref, he's holding me... Ref, he's grabbing my face mask... Ref, he's holding on every play... Ref, if you don't call holding, someone's going to get killed... Ref, Ref, Ref..."

I don't know why someone hasn't told the defensive linemen that holding is legal. Offensive linemen are allowed to grab the defender by the sweater in the chest area as long the player is directly in front of them. John Gregory, a former head coach in both Hamilton and

Saskatchewan said, "If one of my defensive linemen can't get away from a lineman holding his sweater, he doesn't belong in the league."

The only defensive lineman who didn't complain was John Helton, the all-Canadian defensive tackle who played for Calgary and then Winnipeg late in his career, who was constantly held sometimes by two players to keep him away from the quarterback.

I was sure John had a speech impediment and had his tongue removed when he was a child, because no matter how bad it got, he never complained. When John retired, we thought he had the perfect temperament and experience to become a line umpire.

It looked like Don Barker had John convinced to give it a try, and I thought my offer that he would finally get a chance to flag all those offensive linemen who held him for years would do the trick, but he didn't take the bait.

It didn't take long to find out when a lineman was legitimately complaining about being held. For the next couple of plays you would try and catch the culprit, who was always on his best behavior and did nothing. If you continued to watch, inevitably the quarterback would end up dead at your feet, felled by one of the defensive linemen's buddies, while you're trying to catch the holding. Not only did you not catch the holding, but missed the quarterback getting mugged, and now everyone was screaming at you.

Offensive linemen, the biggest hulks on the team with even bigger stomachs, were a completely different breed. They never bothered yelling at the referee, because they were just plain old boys happy rolling around in the mud, thinking about going out for beer after the game, or working on their new holding techniques.

Chris Walby and Miles Gorrell, two Winnipeg tackles, were two of the largest and most infamous offensive linemen in the league. As a supervisor, I would get weekly reports from coaches complaining about their incessant holding, but all the films usually showed were incredible hulks who defensive linemen couldn't get around.

Finally, I went back on the field to see for myself. Walby had a great technique. He would hit out at the defender's shoulders at the snap and let his hands slip outside the shoulders, which was illegal, just doing it long enough to control this opponent, but usually not long enough to get called. Trying to overpower Chris was a waste of time.

Miles was a different story and the officiating staff can take credit for making him an all-star when we had thought we had driven him out of the league. Miles was playing for Montreal and embarrassed the officiating staff with his tactics in one game by leg whipping, tripping, holding and tackling defensive players all over the field. He was using tactics that the World Wrestling Federation hadn't even dreamed about, all without ever being called.

Don Barker was furious when he reviewed the films and instructed Bill Jones, the umpire in Montreal's next game, to make sure there was no repeat of Miles' tactics. By then Miles had further expanded his repertoire but took five penalties and was cut by Montreal the next day. We thought our problems were over, but wouldn't you know it, Hamilton signed him.

To his credit Miles worked his butt off and became a league all-star. When he was an aging veteran in Winnipeg, I got to see him play up close. I finally saw why the defensive man opposite him got so frustrated. Miles was so big, the defender couldn't get around him, and even when he did, it was such a long trip that the quarterback had already released the ball.

Miles Gorrell was a hell of a lineman when he decided to move his feet, but he killed the artificial turf standing in the same place so long. He was also smart enough to know that the referee couldn't look through his back and see what he was doing, which brought cries from the defender that he was being held, or hugged, on every play.

Every once in a while, you knew it was time to call Miles for holding, because the man opposite him had to re-adjust his sweater on every play, because Miles kept trying to pull it over his head, or because Miles was so big that he kept getting his hand caught under his opponent's face mask, leaving the poor man with nothing but a sore neck and a headache.

Inevitably, I'd call Miles for holding, for something we both knew was far less serious than what he was doing on the previous play. I knew when I walked by the huddle he'd be waiting for me, and sure enough he'd raise his head and, still smiling, say "Neil, after what I've been doing, you're not going to start calling me for that shit." Which meant: you made your call, now leave me alone.

Calling Miles for holding had its own special reward. The defense was so happy you finally caught him, they kept quiet for the rest of the quarter.

And there are hundreds more, whether it's the Toronto Gold Dust twins of Joe Krol and Royal Copeland who broke Western hearts in the Grey Cups of the late '40s; or the Alouette combination of Etcheverry to Paterson in the Monreal-Edmonton classic Grey Cups; or Herb Gray of the Bombers and Johnny Bright of the Eskimos destroying each other in the Western finals; or Saskatchewan Rough Riders Ted Urness and Al Benecick opening gigantic holes for George Reid just like they were drawn on the blackboard; or Winnipeg's young guards Kotowich and Piper, who levelled everything when they came around the corner; or Willie Fleming of the Lions and Leo Lewis of the Bombers dancing through entire defenses with skills that couldn't be taught; or Angelo Mosca making a pancake out of the same Willie Fleming; or Eskimo Gizmo Williams's incredible kick returns in the Grey Cups that were a combination of speed, strength and ingenuity; or Russ Jackson taking apart defenses whether he passed or ran; or watching Tony Gabriel catch the winning TD to beat Saskatchewan in the 1976 Cup or Dave Ridgway doing the same to Hamilton with his winning field goal in probably the best of them all, the 1989 Cup. The list goes on.

These men who play the Canadian game invoke special and lasting memories for those who follow the game, memories that are passed from generation to generation and making us all much richer for the experience.

Index